# SAINTS, SINNERS, AND CLICKERS

Love and Loss in The Last of Us

## MATTHEW J. DISTEFANO

All rights reserved. No part of this book may be used or reproduced, stored in a retrieval system, or transmitted in any form or by any means, electronic, mechanical, photocopying, recording, scanning, or otherwise, without written permission from the publisher except in the case of brief quotations embodied in critical articles and reviews. Permission for wider usage of this material can be obtained through Quoir by emailing permission@quoir.com.

Copyright © 2026 by Quoir
First Edition

Scripture quotations are taken from the New Revised Standard Version Updated Edition. Copyright © 2021 National Council of Churches of Christ in the United States of America. Used by permission. All rights reserved worldwide.

Cover Image by Keith Giles
Cover Design & Interior Layout by Matthew J. Distefano

Print ISBN: 978-1-964252-64-3
Electronic ISBN: 978-1-964252-65-0

Printed in the United States of America

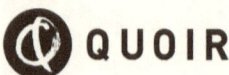

Published by Quoir
Chico, California
www.quoir.com

# TABLE OF CONTENTS

| | |
|---|---|
| Foreword | VII |
| List of Important Characters | XI |
| Preface | XIX |
| Acknowledgments | XXV |
| An Introduction to the End of the World | XXVII |
| 1. Lost in the Darkness | 3 |
| 2. Endure and Survive | 19 |
| 3. Look for the Light | 29 |
| 4. Something to Fight For | 41 |
| 5. No Half Measures | 53 |
| 6. Beyond the Horizon | 65 |
| 7. You Can't Stop This | 79 |
| 8. Okay | 91 |
| 9. It Can't Be for Nothing | 101 |
| 10. You Can't Deny the View | 111 |
| Epilogue | 121 |

Endnotes 127

Bibliography 139

*Dedicated to Lyndsay and Elyse Distefano*

# Foreword

Humans have been imagining the end of the world almost since its beginning. Jewish writers like John of Patmos. Zoroastrian philosophers in Persia. Aztec and Mayan minds in Mesoamerica. The human brain itches, it seems, to know and understand the end.

Interestingly, most of these civilizations would be swept away not from the supernatural judgment or the natural disasters predicted in their stories, but through Man—war, enslavement, and colonization. Fast-forward to apocalyptic stories told by the most recent generations, and you'll find they trend toward these themes of war (nuclear, biochemical, civil, etc.) and enslavement (by disease, extraterrestrial entities, dystopian governments, AI, etc.), and away from the planet-encompassing natural disaster narrative.

Ironic. Maybe a hallmark of a successful apocalyptic narrative is avoiding the era's most likely threat.

But no matter the era, no matter the culture, all apocalyptic narratives grapple with one big of question: *After everything falls apart, what will be left of humanity?*

What parts of us are pure enough to make it through the fire?

Who does the story say is worthy of rescue and preservation, or does the final resolution require a complete wiping away of humanity? And then what will remain?

What will be the last of us?

Although the medium has drastically changed, our modern apocalyptic stories are still wrestling with this same question, but few do it as artfully or resoundingly as *The Last of Us*. When I heard that Matthew was devoting an entire book to exploring the depths of this story, I audibly gasped.

I, too, had spent hours upon hours immersed in the world of Ellie, Joel, Tommy, Tess, Abby, Dina, Jessie, and Lev. And I, too, had never quite gotten over their story.

The book you're holding is the result of the immense research, thought, and courageous vulnerability required to step into a story as weighty as *The Last of Us*, and Matthew has done the work. He is a most capable guide—leading us from the opening scene (Joel's birthday) all the way to the final moments on the beach.

And trust me, we want a guide. Because the story of *The Last of Us* doesn't just wrestle with the archetypal apocalyptic questions pertaining to our survival as a species. It stoops down, crawls close, and wedges itself into the darkest, most terrified places of the individual human heart. True, it allows us to wonder, "What will be the last of us?" But it also prompts us to ask, "What would be the last of *me*?" And rather than give us answers, the story responds with a question of its own: "What would you allow yourself to become for love?" Because herein lies the answer.

We first explore this theme through Joel's story. With the death of Sarah, we watch his personal apocalypse against the backdrop of civilization's death. And what is left after this? What is the last of Joel? A brutal creature, attempting to survive, without the soul pulse he had when Sarah was safe and happy and his. Joel is alive, but in every way that matters, Joel is dead—an adagio on a theme of the infected.

The idea that a foul-mouthed teenage girl would break through the barriers around his soul seems as impossible as the idea of her immunity to the virus destroying the world. And yet, Ellie is our species' last hope. But, more importantly, Ellie is Joel's last hope.

This is when Joel is faced with the question: *"What would you allow yourself to become for love?"* In his rampage through the Fireflies' hospital, Joel is still the brutal killing creature we've come to expect. But it is not bitterness or apathy or a desperate desire to survive that fuels him. This is his answer:

*"For love—for her—I will become ruthless."*

Matthew, like most exceptional fathers, can identify with Joel's instinct here. I am not a father. I am, however, my father's daughter. So, I resonate more easily with Abby. I am also a big sister, and I have been a foster mom, so Abby's movement toward Lev (a young boy, abused, hunted, and vulnerable) strikes a chord in me. If anything, this keeps conversations between Matthew and me interesting.

Throughout *Part II*, we watch as the story asks its question to Ellie, to Tommy, to Dina, to Abby: "What would you allow yourself to become for love?" And we're left to grapple with their choices. Some we cheer, some we lament. None are as painful as the death of Nora, when a single button-press prompt shows us that Ellie has made up her mind: for love, she would become a monster, and we have no choice but to be complicit in that.

And through hours upon hours of gameplay (and re-play), we are looking at the question out of the corner of our eye, "What would I allow myself to become?"

This is why Matthew's guidance is so helpful. The world of Joel, Ellie, and Abby is fraught with horror, heartbreak, and yet, miraculously, beauty. Love, belonging, reconciliation, and meaning still exist if you know where to look. And Matthew does.

I agree with him when he says that *The Last of Us* is one of the most important stories of our time, and we can thank our lucky stars he's committed his knowledge of it to these pages. This is not just a book about a game. It's a book about us—our rage, our resilience, our ruin, and our redemption. And I can't imagine a better guide to walk us through it than Matthew.

We may never stop imagining the end of the world. But if we're lucky, we'll keep discovering and creating stories like *The Last of Us* that help us make sense of who we are, what we love, and what we're willing to become to protect it. I'll leave you to it...

> May your survival be long.
> And may your death be swift.

— **LAUREN CIBENE**
Author of *Tigers in a Lifeboat*

# List of Important Characters

**Abby Anderson**

A former Firefly and daughter of surgeon Jerry Anderson. Abby becomes a WLF soldier after her father's death. Such loss drives her to seek vengeance, but later she undergoes a redemptive arc after forming a bond with Lev, a young Seraphite defector.

**Bill (Last Name Unknown)**

A paranoid, survivalist loner living in Lincoln, Massachusetts. Bill begrudgingly helps Joel and Ellie by providing them with a vehicle. His worldview is deeply cynical, and he values preparedness and autonomy above all else.

**David (Last Name Unknown)**

The charismatic yet predatory leader of a cannibalistic group. Initially presenting as reasonable, David is revealed to be manipulative and violent. He attempts to kill Ellie after she rejects his control and is ultimately killed by her.

## Dina (Last Name Unknown)

Ellie's girlfriend and eventual partner. She accompanies Ellie on her initial journey of vengeance in *Part II* and later gives birth to their son, JJ. Dina represents love, stability, and the life Ellie could have had.

## Ellie Williams

The immune teenager at the center of Parts *I* and *II*. Ellie is sarcastic, smart, and fiercely loyal. Her journey spans from hope to despair, and finally to a painful, quiet form of healing. Her immunity may have saved the world, but she is never given the choice.

## Eugene Linden

An older resident of Jackson and former Firefly. He serves as a mentor figure to Ellie and Tommy and is known for his knowledge of technology and his private stash of contraband, including weed and old video games.

## Frank (Last Name Unknown)

Bill's partner, who grows tired of Bill's controlling behavior and attempts to leave him. Frank is found dead by suicide, having been infected. His relationship with Bill is tragic, marked by love and conflict.

## Henry (Last Name Unknown)

Sam's older brother and caretaker. He and Sam briefly travel with Joel and Ellie. After Sam is bitten and turns, Henry kills his infected brother before taking his own life in despair.

### Isaac Dixon

The authoritarian leader of the WLF in Seattle. A former FEDRA officer, Isaac is ruthless in his tactics, particularly in the war against the Seraphites. His belief in ultimate power ultimately leads to brutal consequences.

### Jesse (Last Name Unknown)

A leader within the Jackson community, Dina's ex-boyfriend and father of JJ. He joins Ellie's mission to Seattle and remains a voice of reason and maturity. Jesse is killed suddenly by Abby during a confrontation.

### Jerry Anderson

A Firefly surgeon and Abby's father. He is tasked with creating a vaccine using Ellie's immunity, which would have required her death. Joel kills him while rescuing Ellie, setting off the events of *Part II*.

### Joel Miller

A smuggler and former father who loses his daughter Sarah on Outbreak Day. Joel becomes Ellie's reluctant guardian, growing to love her deeply, and ultimately dooming humanity to save her life. He is brutally killed by Abby early in *Part II*.

### Jordan (Last Name Unknown)

A WLF soldier who is part of Ellie's enemy roster in *Part II*. He is one of the people responsible for torturing Joel and is later killed by Ellie in Seattle.

## Leah (Last Name Unknown)

A former Firefly turned WLF soldier. She is part of Abby's squad and is found dead in Seattle, having been killed by the Seraphites. Ellie learns of her while hunting down Joel's killers.

## Lev (Last Name Unknown)

A young Seraphite (referred to as "Lily" by his cult), Lev is a transgender boy who flees the Seraphites with his sister, Yara. He forms a strong bond with Abby, becoming her moral compass and giving her purpose beyond vengeance.

## Manny Alvarez

A loyal soldier of the WLF, Manny is a close friend of Abby Anderson. He serves alongside her in Seattle and is known for his charm, humor, and strong moral compass, though his fate is ultimately tragic.

## Maria Miller

Joel's sister-in-law and a leader in the Jackson community. She is pragmatic, protective of those under her care, and often clashes with Joel and Tommy about the risks they take.

## Marlene (Last Name Unknown)

The leader of the Fireflies and a close friend of Ellie's mother, Anna. Marlene is who ultimately orders the surgery that would kill Ellie. She is killed by Joel after begging him to let her live.

## Mel (Last Name Unknown)

A WLF medic and Owen's girlfriend. Mel is compassionate but disapproves of Abby's brutality. She is pregnant during the events of *Part II* and is killed by Ellie during her hunt for Joel's killers.

## Owen Moore

A former Firefly and member of the WLF, Owen is Abby's ex-boyfriend and Mel's partner. He becomes disillusioned with the WLF's violence and seeks peace. He is killed by Ellie in Seattle.

## Riley Abel

A rebellious teenager and Ellie's best friend, Riley briefly joins the Fireflies before reuniting with Ellie in "Left Behind." Their bond is deep and eventually romantic, but their time together ends in tragedy when both are bitten by the infected. Riley dies offscreen, her loss leaving a lasting impact on Ellie.

## Robert (Last Name Unknown)

A small-time arms dealer in Boston who betrays Joel and Tess. He is killed early in *Part I* after a failed weapons deal. His death leads Joel and Tess to meet Ellie.

## Sam (Last Name Unknown)

Henry's younger brother. Sam is a cheerful, curious boy who is bitten by an infected. He hides the bite, turns overnight, and is killed by Henry, who then takes his own life.

## Sarah Miller

Joel's teenage daughter, killed by a soldier on Outbreak Day. Her death profoundly shapes Joel's character and motivates much of his behavior throughout *Part I*.

## Seth (Last Name Unknown)

A minor character in Jackson who insults Ellie and Dina for kissing in public. He later apologizes, under pressure from Maria. His character highlights lingering prejudice even in seemingly peaceful communities.

## Seraphite Prophet (Also known as "The Prophet" or "The Woman")

The deceased spiritual leader of the radical religious group, the Seraphites. During her life, she preaches nonviolence and simplicity, but her teachings are later distorted into a cultic ideology after her death.

## Shimmer

Ellie's horse during the events of *Part II*. Shimmer provides transportation in early parts of the game but is killed in an ambush during the Seattle chapter.

## Tess Servopoulos

Joel's smuggling partner in Boston. Tess is tough, pragmatic, and willing to make morally ambiguous decisions. She sacrifices herself after being bitten, buying Joel and Ellie time to escape.

**Tommy Miller**

Joel's younger brother and a former Firefly. Tommy settles in Jackson and later joins Ellie in seeking revenge against Abby. He becomes increasingly bitter and physically impaired following Joel's death.

**Yara (Last Name Unknown)**

Lev's older sister and a former Seraphite. Protective and self-sacrificial, Yara is mortally wounded during their escape and eventually dies during a confrontation with WLF forces, enabling Lev and Abby to flee.

# PREFACE

Like most elder Millennials, I played my first video game back in the '80s—what my Gen Z daughter calls "the late 1900s." *Ouch.* Though I'm a bit of a stoner and apparently as ancient as they come, I can somehow still vaguely remember experiencing the joy of both *Pole Position* and *Joust* from my stepdad's family room in the Santa Cruz Mountains over thirty years ago. The console du jour? The Atari 7800.

Okay, so I guess I *am* old...

Can I say I was initially hooked on video games? Not quite. A Nintendo Entertainment System ("NES" for real fans) hadn't graced my family's home yet; but boy oh boy, when it did, I was all in! *Super Mario Bros. Tecmo Super Bowl. Contra.*[1] And my God... the 1989 classic *Teenage Mutant Ninja Turtles*. To this day, all these titles are still in my top ten of all time.

Fast forward some thirty-odd years, and while video games have undergone major changes, their basic premise is the same. *Video games are meant to transport us to a world that is not ours.* In the '80s and '90s, we strapped on cleats and tried to tackle an in-form Barry Sanders or Christian Okoye. When we were not busy busting our butts on the gridiron, we put shells on our backs to save April O'Neil from The Shredder, Bebop and Rocksteady, and any other dumb motherfucker who dared get in our way. Other times we fortified with some 'shrooms—not that kind, and certainly not *Cordyceps* either—before questing to rescue Princess Peach from Bowzer. And on many late-night occasions, we even snagged the almighty spread gun to halt the Red Falcon terrorist organization from destroying humanity (all without the iconic thirty-life cheat code if you're a bad-ass like me).

Yeah, those were good times…

What video games did *not* do back then, however, is give us stories like the one we find in *The Last of Us* series. How could they? These were the Wild West days of console entertainment. Graphics were based on "bits"—the OG Nintendo (NES) was 8-bit, Super Nintendo (SNES) was 16-bit, Nintendo 64 (N64) was, you guessed it, 64-bit, and so on. Moreover, there were no voice actors[2] or motion capturing like there is today, so stories were a bit of a non-starter. Also, budgets were hilariously miniscule.[3]

Now, however, a gamer needs to learn a new language just to decipher the graphical capabilities of the various consoles. For instance, the Base Model PlayStation 5 specs read like this: Custom AMD RDNA 2 GPU with 36 complete units, 10.28 TFLOPs, 16 GB GDDR6 RAM, supporting 4K resolution, ray tracing, high frame rates, and checkerboard-style upscaling, with 4K 120Hz, HDMI 2.1 output. The Pro Model obviously ramps up the technology, but unless you are a tech geek, it's all just gobbledygook at this point. When it comes to voice acting and motion capturing, making a game is essentially like making a movie—only harder—with budgets that can approach half a billion US dollars.[4]

Does this mean modern video games are better than the classics? No, it just means the bar is significantly higher. Whether a game developer reaches such heights is determined by several factors. One thing is for certain, however: Neil Druckmann and the team at Naughty Dog hit the highest of highs and delivered on what is, for me, *the greatest story ever told in a video game*. The icing on the cake is that the games themselves are fun as hell to play, even when the story is less than fun to experience.

Speaking of the story, though, while it should be obvious that there are spoilers ahead—how could I even write a book about *The Last of Us* without spoiling the story?—I would be remiss not to make such a disclaimer *perfectly* explicit. So, here it goes: SPOILER ALERT.

There. You've been warned.

Truth be told, *The Last of Us* will make you scream at the top of your lungs while also leaving you breathless and speechless at the same time. Within the first fifteen minutes, the game leads you to the gates of hell, looks you square in the eyes, and heartlessly kicks you in, locking the bolt behind you.[5] As you watch Joel experience the death of his teenage daughter in real time, you are left in utter shambles: "What in the actual fuck have I gotten myself into?" is what I remember asking during my first playthrough.

Again, this is just within the first fifteen minutes of the game. The Prologue. The initial "hook." The beginning of the brutal journey you are, for some reason or another, choosing to embark on (a big ask for any gamer, let alone a parent).

As the father of a teenage daughter, I cannot put into words the hell Joel must have felt that day. Not only losing a child, but being helpless as their life fades in front of you, is an experience no parent should ever have to face. And yet, here we are, time after time, picking up the controller and choosing to step foot through the threshold of the hellish universe that is *The Last of Us* to experience perdition alongside a man so broken it's a wonder he didn't "end it all" long before the story even begins.[6]

This reality forces me to ask: Why do we choose to play a game like this? Simple. Because, even though video games tend to transport us to a whole new world, some of the best represent real life. They represent the human experience. We've all faced loss of some kind, even if not to the degree Joel does. We've also tasted love and all the beauty and tragedy that come from it. So, in a very real way, Joel's messy story is our messy story. Joel's morally ambiguous universe is our morally ambiguous universe. And no amount of running from such a reality will ever change the fact that the contradictory world of *The Last of Us* is our contradictory world.

As we progress through this book, it will become quite clear what I mean by such a statement, so there is no need to get too far ahead of ourselves just yet. For now, allow me to get a few housekeeping items out of the way before striking at the heart of what this book is all about.

First, I write this without knowing if there will be a *The Last of Us: Part III*. As it stands, there is no mention of production, and all we are left with are veiled hints, which, in typical Neil Druckmann style, have been exceptionally ambiguous. For instance, in the documentary, *Grounded II: The Making of The Last of Us Part II*, he initially states:

> The first game had such a clean concept of the unconditional love a parent feels for their child. The second one, once we landed on this idea of the pursuit of justice at any cost—justice for the ones you love—it felt like there's a clean concept here and there's a through-line from the first game about love. If we never get to do it again, this is a fine ending point and the last bite of the apple. The story's done [...] I've been thinking about, "Is there a concept there?" And for years now, I haven't been able to find that concept. But recently that's changed. I don't have a story, but I do have a concept that, to me, is as exciting as *I*, as exciting as *II*, is its own thing, but has this through-line through all three. So, it does feel like there's probably one more chapter to this story.[7]

Months later, however, Druckmann says *this* to *Variety*: "I guess the only thing I would say is don't bet on there being more 'Last of Us.' This could be it."[8]

Nevertheless, if there is a *Part III*, I can assure you that I will write a follow-up after the publication of this book. Whether my analysis will result in another full title or just an addendum to this book remains to be seen, and it will depend on what transpires during what would assuredly be the final chapter of the story.

Second, to the critics who believe that folks like myself should refrain from analyzing tales such as these for fear of tainting or cheapening them, allow me to say that my experience on the matter so far has been the opposite. As someone who has always loved *The Lord of the Rings*, writing three books on the topic has only led me and my readers to fall deeper in love with Middle-earth, Hobbits, and all things Tolkien.[9] Likewise, as I have prepared for this book, I've never felt closer to Joel and Ellie, nor more fearful of the clickers and hunters who desire to kill them. My hope is that you will feel the same thing as you progress through this book.

Third, when it comes to the canonicity of *The Last of Us*, while I consider the HBO series to indeed be a welcome addition to the series, I will primarily be referring to the events of the video games. At times, I may refer to the television show, but only to enhance the conversation at hand. Any contradictory bits of information—such as the manner in which Frank dies, or the fact that in Season 1 of the show there are no contagious fungal spores—will be omitted from this book for the sake of clarity and cohesiveness.

Finally—and I am sure you all know this by now—some of the themes of the game (and as such, the book you have in your hands) are quite heavy and are likely to be hugely triggering to some. So, please be aware of this and only bite off as much as you can chew (pun intended). If things get too burdensome, take a break and come back *when* or *if* you are able. One theme of the game is the effects of trauma on mental health, so make sure to always care for yourself and seek peace of mind in all that you do.

With that said, I hope those who are ready to dive headlong into this brutal world will strap in and get ready for a ruthless ride that covers the full spectrum of human emotion. From love and loss, to tragedy and hope, to corny puns and even low-brow cum jokes, *The Last of Us* has everything needed for a great story.[10] In this book, I hope to show why this tale is one of the greatest of all time, even when it rips our hearts straight out of our fucking chests.

For those willing and able, I look forward to pressing on with you. Let's make sure to keep our boots dry, our wits sharp, and to watch each other's six. We never know when we'll come across a clicker, or perhaps worse yet, other human survivors.

And lastly, *may we always find something to fight for... no matter what.*[11]

— **MATTHEW J. DISTEFANO**
September 19, 2025
Chico, California

# Acknowledgments

If writing this book was a trek across post-pandemic America, then these are the people who walked beside me through every overgrown street and abandoned checkpoint:

First, to my wife, Lyndsay: you are the light in the darkness, the fire that never goes out. I could wander the wasteland a thousand times and still come home to you.

To Elyse, my daughter, my joy, my everything, my reminder that beauty always finds a way to grow: thank you for keeping me grounded even as I'm lost in fictional apocalypses.

To Michael Machuga, my best friend and fellow survivor: thank you for the endless late-night chats about philosophy, theology, and which Hobbit we most resonate with. You've always had my back, and whether we're planting a row of Brandywine tomatoes or arguing over metaphysics, I just enjoy being in your company.

Keith Giles: you've been more than just a business partner at Quoir or a podcasting comrade-in-arms. You're family. Thanks for always being willing to dive into dangerous theological territory with me, even when the evangelical clickers are closing in.

To Crystal Kuld, my editor and guide: your work on this manuscript was like a perfectly timed Molotov in a room full of bloaters. Sharp, fiery, and exactly what was needed.

To Andy Colenzo: thank you for showing me what reconciliation truly looks like. Our journey has been a gift even amidst the years of radio silence. You remind me that healing is messy, but possible.

Michelle Collins: thank you for your unwavering friendship and support. Whether it's personal or professional, you show up. That matters more than you know.

To Lauren Cibene: your foreword is beautiful, and your words honor this project with a depth that elevates everything that follows. Thank you.

To every single person who has supported me on Patreon, bought a book, or listened to *Heretic Happy Hour*: you're like a group of Fireflies in my corner, always searching for the light. This book wouldn't exist without you.

And finally, to the fans of *The Last of Us*: you get it. You know that this story isn't just about infected monsters or grizzled protagonists. It's about us, about what we cling to when everything falls apart, about who we become when love and loss collide. This book is for you.

Endure and survive.

# An Introduction to the End of the World

*September 26, 2013—Outbreak Day*

Originating from South America through fungal-tainted crops, the *Cordyceps* brain infection (CBI)—a parasitic contagion caused by the *Cordyceps* fungus—becomes a near-instant pandemic as it ferociously spreads throughout the entire human population, reaching Austin, Texas, and other US cities in the early morning hours of September 27, 2013. According to an article in the *Texas Herald* entitled, "FDA expands the list of contaminated crops. Massive recalls anticipated," the origin of the infection is clear:

> The Food and Drug Administration's investigation of crops potentially tainted with mold continues across the country. Initial lists distributed to vendors nationwide warned against crops imported from South America, but now the scope has extended to include Central America and Mexico. Several companies have already voluntarily recalled their food products from the shelves.[1]

(According to a 2015 World Health Organization report, within months of the onset of the infection, roughly 60% of the world's population had either died from or are infected by the *Cordyceps* brain infection.[2])

Declaring a nationwide state of emergency after being unable to slow the rate of spread across the population, the United States government deploys the military and shuts down major highways, setting up camps for uninfected residents to flee to for safety. In Austin, many of the infected escape a local hospital, and, because of the nature of the *Cordyceps* infection, begin attacking city residents who are trapped due to the unusually high volume of traffic.

Catastrophes such as the one in Austin become commonplace across the nation, leading the Federal Disaster Response Agency (FEDRA) to seize control of the government and set up quarantine zones (QZs). The agency quickly enacts martial law and descends into a tyrannical police state. Within the walls of these QZs, citizens are subjected to forced labor,[3] food rationings,[4] and all manners of civil rights violations. For example, to prevent overcrowding in Pittsburgh, civilians are murdered by the hundreds or even thousands.[5] In Boston, large areas are carpet bombed to create "buffer zones" between the QZs and the infected.[6] Throughout the nation, zero-tolerance Mycotoxin Containment Protocols are enacted and soldiers with searchlights guard 30-foot-high towers, shooting anyone deemed a threat, including residents of all stripes—men, women, *and* children. Because of these extreme measures, by 2033 FEDRA all but collapses under the weight of its autocracy and is reduced to governing only a small number of cities, most notably Boston. By the time of the events of *The Last of Us*, FEDRA comprises the final remnant of the United States government (alongside the Department of Defense and the Centers for Disease Control[7]). Dubbed "fascists" by the Washington Liberation Front (WLF), the agency is challenged by multiple resistance groups across the former United States.

## A NEW WORLD ORDER

Within the walls of the Quarantine Zones—no matter the city—life is harsh. While it is true that the infected are often kept at bay, citizens within the QZs are by no means thriving. As such, paramilitary and militia groups like the Fireflies rise to prominence as an alternative. Terrorists according to some, freedom fighters to others, the Fireflies revolt against FEDRA in multiple locations, hoping to restore the former constitutional republic. However, their mission is largely unsuccessful as the Fireflies eventually disband and are forced to withdraw to the island of Catalina by the end of the events of *Part II*.

Other militia groups such as the Washington Liberation Front (WLF, or "Wolves"), employ tactics similar to those of the Fireflies—sabotage, propaganda, and guerilla warfare—which yields mixed results. In the Seattle QZ, for instance, the WLF finds success in overthrowing FEDRA, but experiences difficulty in their broader war against the Washingtonian Seraphites (a rigid religious order from Seattle's Lower Queen Anne suburb). In Southern California, hunter groups like the Rattlers fill the void left behind by a pre-pandemic government. Across the country—in places like Pittsburgh and Kansas City—similar groups ruthlessly control everything in their immediate vicinity.

On the other hand, more peaceful communities such as Jackson, Wyoming also spring to life. Under the watchful leadership of Maria Miller, Jackson becomes a vestige of what once was—communal and "regular"—proving that post-pandemic life could loosely resemble what it was prior to 2013, even if on the smallest of scales.

### The Fireflies

In addition to fighting FEDRA across the nation, the Fireflies spend numerous years and copious amounts of energy trying to find a cure for the *Cordyceps* brain infection. Among the physicians in charge of developing a vaccine is surgeon Dr. Jerry Anderson, father of WLF soldier, Abby Anderson. Led by their respected yet somewhat cold leader, Marlene, at its height the group consists of at least 318 registrants,[8] many of whom would die prior to the end of the events of *Part II*.

On April 28, 2034, a Firefly patrol discovers Joel and Ellie (the chief protagonists of *Part I*) in the tunnels near their headquarters in Salt Lake City. After being taken to Marlene, Joel discovers that Ellie has been prepped for the surgery that will supposedly save humanity, but that she has no chance of survival. This prompts Joel to massacre every Firefly, including Marlene and Dr. Anderson, which leads to the group's formal disbanding. However, years later, Abby will learn that over 200 former members have taken refuge on Catalina Island, just miles off the coast of California.

## The Washington Liberation Front (WLF)

"May your survival be long. May your death be swift," says the Washington Liberation Front.[9] Like the Fireflies, the WLF begins as a resistance movement against FEDRA's brutal control. Initiated by Emma and Jason Patterson, the WLF is quickly deemed a terrorist organization and as such, most of their leadership is eliminated through FEDRA's zero-tolerance policies. By the time of the events of *Part II*, former Marine Isaac Dixon is the only surviving member of the rebellion's original leadership.

After suffering weeks of violent attacks against their strongholds, FEDRA leader Lt. Torres counters WLF's growing aggression by opening fire on all protests—peaceful and otherwise—culminating in the Thursday Market Massacre, an event that leads to a spike in WLF support across the city of Seattle.[10] The incident is so brutal, it even causes some FEDRA soldiers to defect and join the militia group.

In time, FEDRA loses much of their support and are forced to evacuate the city. However, due to a timely tip from an informant, the WLF is ready to spring a trap. The FEDRA soldiers who are not slaughtered on the highway leading out of town are chased into a nearby courthouse and massacred en masse, thereby ending FEDRA's reign over the city.[11]

With FEDRA out of the way, the WLF establishes dominance in Seattle, setting up its own form of martial law, which forces all civilians to pledge allegiance to the group. Deemed criminals and fascists by several residents, many come to view the WLF as worse rulers than even FEDRA.[12] Over the years, the WLF become increasingly leery of anyone deemed "outsiders," which leads to an all-out war against a religious group known as the Seraphites (derogatorily called "Scars" by WLF members[13]).

The genesis of the war against the Seraphites is not unlike the many skirmishes the WLF has engaged in with FEDRA. After the Seraphite leader, known only as "the Prophet," bombs a WLF platoon, all-out war ensues. Over time, countless atrocities on both sides are committed, peace treaties are broken, and by the onset of the events of *Part II*, neither side has relented.

## The Salt Lake Crew

The Salt Lake Crew is an informal name for a group of former Fireflies who end up joining the WLF after the killing of Dr. Jerry Anderson, the surgeon who was to operate on Ellie toward the end of *Part I*.

Alongside Abby (Dr. Anderson's daughter) is Owen Moore (Abby's then boyfriend), Nora Harris and Mel (two interns studying under Dr. Anderson), Manny Alvarez (a soldier from Mexico), and Jordan, Nick, and Leah, who all make up the group that would eventually exact revenge against Joel for the killing of the surgeon. During the events of *Part II*, everyone except Abby is killed, either by Ellie and Tommy, or in a skirmish with the Seraphites.

## The Seraphites

Sometime between September 2013 and March 2014, in the Lower Queen Anne suburb of Seattle, the Seraphites, known pejoratively as "Scars" by those in the WLF, are founded by an individual known only as "the Prophet." As a primitivist cultish faction, the Seraphites have vowed to live entirely off the land, reject technology, and lead an egalitarian lifestyle. Like all doomsday religions, they see CBI as a punishment for humanity's sins.

Prior to their war with the Washington Liberation Front, the Seraphites engage in acts of terror against the residents of Seattle. As a local resident's final note written to her husband, Simon, reads:

> I hope you never read this note. I hope I can crumple it up, burn it, when you return to us. It's been... I don't even know how many hours since you left. I went out to look for you and these hooded people spotted me. They shouted at me, called me a sinner, then started shooting. I ran back in and barricaded the door. All I can hear is the rain, but I'm worried they're still out there. Should I run? Should I stay? I feel completely paralyzed. I'm sorry I got so sick. I'm sorry I let you go to the hospital by yourself. I'm sorry I didn't stay hidden like you told me. If anything happens to me, I want you to know how much I love you. Please come back. I'm so scared.[14]

Both Paige and Simon go on to die from their wounds inflicted by the Seraphites,[15] who become known for their brutal sacrificial practices—something not originally taught by the prophet.[16]

As time passes, the Seraphites end up facing persecution at the hands of the WLF, which leads to escalated tensions between the two groups. The hostilities reach a boiling point after the WLF executes the prophet—being deemed "too dangerous" by WLF leader, Isaac Dixon.

After years of fighting—each faction suffering significant losses—the two groups finally come to a truce. The accord is short-lived, however, with conflicting reports as to how the war has become rekindled.[17] Nevertheless, the fighting continues, off and on, through the events of *Part II*. The war ends after the Seraphites hold off a WLF assault on their island, though not before nearly every home and building are razed to the ground.

## The Rattlers

Like many of the militia groups who take control of various locales after the CBI outbreak, the Rattlers are a faction of ruthless slavers known primarily for their brutality. Unlike the peaceful community of Jackson, Wyoming, the Rattlers secure their place in the world (Santa Barbara, California) by enslaving unsuspecting passersby, even going so far as to purposefully infect them solely for entertainment. Those who resist enslavement or attempt to escape the camps are sent to "the pillars"—wooden beams set out on the beach used to slowly torture victims prior to their deaths.

Toward the end of the events of *Part II*, the prisoners of the slave camps are let out by Ellie, who then take to assaulting the Rattlers before engulfing their base in flames and killing most of the men.

## The Jackson Community

Unlike every community encountered by Ellie and Joel, the people of Jackson, Wyoming are a welcoming and friendly group. Founded after the onset of the CBI outbreak, Jackson is a self-sustaining community that more or less attempts to follow a way of life like that of pre-pandemic America. The town draws its power from a nearby hydroelectric dam, has established gardens and greenhouses, livestock ranches for meat, eggs, and poultry, and a thriving downtown where merchants communistically trade and barter for goods and services. Children and families are even able to enjoy movie nights and live in relative peace.

Due to an increase in encounters with the infected, multiple patrols roam the countryside outside Jackson, clearing any hordes they come across. By 2039, however, Jackson faces its greatest challenge as its most competent and proficient patrolmen have either been killed (Joel, Eugene, and Jesse) or have retired (Dina and Tommy).

## THE CORDYCEPS BRAIN INFECTION (CBI)

As we have already established, the *Cordyceps* brain infection (CBI) is a mutated strain of the *Cordyceps* fungus that originates in South America through infected crops. By the end of 2013, according to World Health Organization, nearly 60% of the world's population has either died or become infected with CBI.[18] The contagion is spread, not only through tainted crops, but from the bites of other infected hosts,[19] as well as fungal spores that are released by the deceased.

The *Cordyceps* brain infection grows in four distinct stages, keeping its host alive throughout the entire process. During Stage One, which begins within two days of infection, the host loses all higher brain function, becoming exceedingly violent and aggressive in the process. After two weeks, the host begins losing the ability to see as the fungus continues to grow over their head and eyes. This is considered Stage Two. Stage Three begins a year after infection. With the host completely blind, the fungus adapts to using a form of echolocation—a series of clicks that aids them in navigating though the world. Stage Four, though rare, begins a decade into the infection and involves hardened plates that cover most of the host's body. Below is information taken from a flyer distributed to the residents of Seattle by FEDRA during the initial stages of the pandemic:

**INFECTED STAGE 1**

*Cordyceps* has taken over the victim's motor functions. Fast and agile, Stage 1 infected usually travel in packs. DO NOT LET THEM SWARM YOU.

## INFECTED STAGE 2

Uses environment to hide and ambush victims. Will frequently flank and attack from behind. Approach with caution and check your surroundings.

## INFECTED STAGE 3

Completely blind, acute hearing, uses echolocation to seek out prey. Keep your distance. Stage 3 infected are known for their ferocious attacks and are extremely lethal.

## INFECTED STAGE 4

Rare but dangerous evolution of stage 3 infected. Incredibly strong and capable of throwing acidic projectiles. DO NOT ENGAGE UNLESS ABSOLUTELY NECESSARY.

Once the fungal infection kills the host, the body develops long stalks that release infectious spores.

### Stage One: Runners

People who are exposed to *Cordyceps* will begin to "turn" within two days. The first signs and symptoms of CBI include increased aggression and hostility toward others, pale skin, thinning hair, and painful lesions. Stage One "runners" tend to clumsily attack non-infected individuals in hordes, though some only do so when first confronted. Although it is not scientifically proven, some believe that while in this Stage humans retain a semblance of their agency, though it is largely stunted. For instance, on one occasion, a runner can be seen crying after killing and eating one of their friends, suggesting remorse amidst an inability to control one's actions.[20]

## Stage Two: Stalkers

As the disease progresses, the host begins to develop large fungal growths on their head and face, which begin to cover their eyes. Like runners, Stage Two infected retain some of their human characteristics, but begin to use echolocation as they stalk their potential victims—hence the colloquial term "stalkers."

## Stage Three: Clickers

After approximately a year of infection, most hosts have completely lost their ability to see; instead, they use a rudimentary form of echolocation to search for potential victims. Unlike runners and stalkers, these "clickers" have developed physical strength that is vastly superior to that of the average person. Most of their human features are gone: their skin and eyes covered by scaly fungal growth, their teeth missing or jagged, and their face split open and scarred. If a clicker discovers a potential victim, they will enter an all-out-assault mode that can easily overwhelm even the strongest human survivor.

## Stage Four: Bloaters and Shamblers

Commonly referred to as "bloaters," Stage Four infected are covered in thick, bioluminescent fungal scales that protect them from even the most powerful weapons. Additionally, bloaters possess mycotoxin pouches they can remove to bombard potential victims with. Though their echolocation is less precise than that of clickers, bloaters are difficult to dispatch as they use their dominating physical strength to overwhelm anyone caught in their grasp.

A second variety of Stage Four infected known as "shamblers" can be discovered in watery locations like Seattle. Like bloaters, shamblers can endure massive amounts of damage due to the fungal growths covering their bodies. However, in rainier or more humid areas, these advanced infected have also developed pustules that release toxic acid. In addition to their oversized heads and torsos, their mouths are stuck in a fully gaped position, making them unable to bite their victims. However, due to their overwhelming strength and size, they can rip survivors apart with ease.

**The Rat King**

The Rat King is the name given to the most enigmatic infected encountered in *The Last of Us* universe. Discovered in the basement of Lakehill Seattle Hospital, the Rat King is a beastly entity composed of multiple stalkers, clickers, and a bloater, all "fused" together by the *Cordyceps* fungus. According to WLF member, Nora Harris, the Rat King is likely the result of some of the earliest infected being trapped together in the hospital and is the only known case of a conjoined infected.

## NATURE FINDS A WAY

Although the world of *The Last of Us* is an unforgiving one wrought with peril, the natural beauty cannot be denied. Indeed, there is a strange, almost sacred allure in watching the world reclaim itself, where no matter the locale, vestiges of civilization and culture are wrapped in flora and fauna, striking a chord that is simultaneously unnerving and serene.[21]

In this world, nature is no longer tamed, domesticated, or paved over. It has broken through the asphalt of humanity's ambitions and swallowed whole the scaffolding of our empires. Skyscrapers lean like tired elders, covered in moss, lichen, and ivy. Streets once choked with exhaust and the honking horns of an impatient workforce now host deer, rabbits, and even the occasional tower of giraffes. Rusted out cars become planters. Strip malls rot. Trees burst through living room floors.

Ironic, isn't it? That humanity's collapse is the catalyst for the planet's healing.[22] While the mutated *Cordyceps* fungus is a grotesque perversion of natural life—a parasitic tour de force that puppets the living into death—it is also a reminder that nature isn't sentimental. It evolves, adapts, and reclaims.

We like to think of ourselves as the protagonists of Earth's story, but in this world, we are just another invasive species in need of substantial pruning. Between the concrete and the capitalism, the prodigious skyscrapers and the political systems, nothing is permanent. They are but temporary illusions of control, undone in a matter of days by something microscopic and ancient.

But this isn't just a story of devastation; it's a story of resurrection. Not of humanity—at least not yet—but of the wild. And in the wild, borders and agendas are laid bare for the façades they are. In the wild, everything just is. In a world where faith has crumbled and institutions lie in ruin, the most enduring truth may be the one written in vines—sprouting through decay, whispering that even at the end of the world, life always finds a way, even if it doesn't feature, or include, any of us.

## BEYOND SURVIVAL
## What's Left to Lose? What's Left to Save?

With the backdrop to *The Last of Us* now firmly in our minds, let us set the stage for the remainder of this book.

As much as the story of Ellie and Joel is one of survival, it is not really about that. Not in the way we typically think. It's not about outlasting the infected or dodging raiders or crafting enough shivs to get through the next locked door, though those things are important. *The Last of Us* is primarily about what survival and the fear of death[23] does to us. All of us. Our minds. Our morals. Our relationships. Indeed, our very souls.

This is a story soaked in grief and aching with memory. It's one long meditation on what it means to love and to lose, to hope and to hate, to kill and to carry on. It's also a story that refuses to give in to the easy and reductive answers, instead opting to inundate us with contradiction and paradox. There are no saints here, but perhaps very few truly evil sinners either. There are only wounded and desperate people doing the best they can with whatever tattered sense of right and wrong they have managed to hold onto. Or let go of.

In the pages that follow, we are going to explore this world not just as gamers or fans, but as philosophers, theologians, ethicists, and even poets and musicians. We'll ask questions that rarely have cut-and-dried answers:

- Do we have free will, or are we just products of our trauma and our tribe?
- Is vengeance ever just, or is it just violence with better PR?
- Can love save us, or does it damn us to a life of suffering?
- Can a lie be moral? Can the truth be a weapon?
- What does redemption look like when no one's innocent, and no one is left unscarred?

All in all, what we want to explore and evaluate is this: *What does it mean to be human at the end of the world?*

We will wrestle with the death of the proverbial "good guy," the ambiguity of morality, and the theological implications of a universe seemingly devoid of divine intervention. We will talk about sin, sanctity, survival, and sacrifice, and we'll do so with the full weight of nuance strapped over our shoulder. Because *The Last of Us* demands it.

So come, let us wander through the ruins of a broken but blossoming world. Let us listen to the silence between ear-splitting gunshots. Let us follow the trail of pain and beauty that Ellie and Joel, Abby and Dina, and so many others have left behind. Not because we are trying to escape our world of beauty and pain, but because maybe by understanding their world, we will develop a better understanding of ours. Because in the end, their world is our world. Their story is our story. We are all saints and sinners. We are all the last of us.

# 1

# LOST IN THE DARKNESS

*Finding Meaning in the Apocalypse*

"*When you're lost in the darkness, look for the light.*"

— **THE FIREFLIES' SLOGAN**

Humanity has been enamored with apocalyptic literature for thousands of years. The earliest known apocalypses are Jewish works that can be dated between 200 BCE to 165 BCE. Contrary to some later narratives emphasizing a literal end-of-the-world scenario, the most ancient Jewish writers did not conceive of their stories in eschatological terms. During the revolt of the Maccabees, however, a more pessimistic view of the present world began to dominate their minds, which caused a shift in the apocalyptic mindset and eventually led to the creation of the *end of days* scenario we are all now familiar with.

Fast forward thousands of years, and perhaps tens of thousands of apocalyptic writings later, and we arrive at *The Last of Us*. More than a video game or subsequent television adaptation, this tale is not unlike the many apocalypses that have come before but is enigmatic in its ability to see just how far our physical, emotional, *and* spiritual boundaries can be stretched. In other words, this story does what any good apocalyptic tale does, only better.

In *The Last of Us*, we bear witness to the depths to which the *Cordyceps* brain infection drives humanity, but the pandemic is far from a literal, monster-centric end-of-the-world narrative. Indeed, the runners, stalkers, clickers, bloaters, and shamblers provide only half the horror, and are far too zombie-like to be our gravest concern. As Bill admits to Joel, "as bad as those things are, at least they're predictable. It's the normal people that scare me."[1] Undoubtedly, the worst of the apocalyptic aftermath is what becomes of *us*—human survivors and factions less predictable than the infected, and therefore much more dangerous.

If the infected are the monsters we expect, the survivors are the monsters we fear we might become. The *Cordyceps* outbreak may be the catalyst, but the true apocalypse unfolds in the choices people make once the world ends. *Who do you save when everyone needs saving? Who do you become when all the old laws, rules, and customs collapse?* These are the types of questions this story dares to ask and refuses to answer clearly.

There is no grand narrative of divine rescue here, no *deus ex machina*,[2] no messianic figure who swoops in to save the day. At "the end of all things"[3]—to borrow the words of Frodo Baggins—there is no judgment day that sets the world right. Society ends not with a trumpet blast[4] but with the silent spread of mutated fungal spores, and all that is left is what people are willing to endure. But survival in *The Last of Us* is not merely a matter of food, water, clothing, and shelter; rather, it serves as a moral crucible testing the limits of empathy and loyalty, all the while challenging what it means to remain human in a world that punishes such virtues.

This is one instance where *The Last of Us* separates itself from many of the apocalypses of old: while ancient texts often provide a human-centric cosmic rationale—divine judgment,[5] karmic balance,[6] or a coming new age set to rights by a son of God[7]—this story offers no such comfort.[8] It rejects the idea that suffering necessarily *means something* or that salvation can be seen and tasted (but only on the other side of catastrophe). As Clint Wesley Jones states in his essay, "Joel's Choice: Apocalyptic Fantasies, Dystopian Hope, and the Post-Human Question":

> There are many similarities between *The Last of Us* and other apocalyptic tales, but the significance of *The Last of Us* is that it doesn't ask us to think of how we would rebuild the world into something better. Rather, it asks us to consider how we're going to inhabit a post-apocalyptic world in which we're not the most dominant force for change.[9]

This is a story soaked in ambiguity, where morality shifts like the ruins of cities overgrown with moss and lichen, and the closest thing to a guiding principle is found in a slogan hastily graffitied on a wall: "When you're lost in the darkness, look for the light." That haunting line, echoed throughout the series, captures both the longing and the irony embedded in the narrative. For even when our favorite characters are searching for the light, they often find only shadow. Still, as if balancing on a knife's edge,[10] those who endure continue to search. And *that* search—for meaning, morality, and purpose in a world that has lost all three—is what places *The Last of Us* firmly in the long, tortured lineage of apocalyptic literature.

## THE END OF THE WORLD AS THE END OF MEANING

> "This is the way the world ends,
> not with a bang but a whimper."
>
> — **T.S. ELIOT**, *The Hollow Men*

The word "apocalypse" comes from the Greek word *apokalypsis* (ἀποκάλυψις), meaning "an unveiling" or "uncovering." More than a mere catastrophic event—and not even necessarily a word that should carry with it a negative connotation—an apocalypse is simply a revelation that strips away illusion and exposes the truth that lies beneath. For the Apostle Paul, the apocalypse of God is revealed in the person of Jesus of Nazareth, while Chinese Buddhism revels in a future messianic figure called Maitreya who will one day usher in a new age of enlightenment. In the world of *The Last of Us*, however, what is unveiled is not divine glory or hidden wisdom. What is revealed is rot. It is ruin. It is the slow, fungal decay of everything humanity has used to fashion the world—our cities, our relationships, even our sense of right and wrong. This apocalypse does not descend like fire from heaven, as it did for the Jewish prophet Elijah; it blooms in the soil, rises with the spores, and creeps into the minds and bodies of everything it touches, destroying all meaning in the process.

## The Literal and Metaphorical Apocalypse

As we discussed in the introduction to this book, the literal end of the world begins in September, 2013, with the *Cordyceps* outbreak—a mutation of a parasitic fungus that leaps into humans, turning the infected into hollowed-out husks driven by the singular instinct to spread. Society collapses not in a single spectacular moment of fire and ash, but like a building that crumbles floor by floor. Hospitals overflow. Governments falter. News broadcasts go dark. The world ends in the way a candle burns out... slowly, then suddenly.

But this mycological process is more than just some monster *du jour*. It is a metaphor. It is the poetry of Charles Bukowski written in mildew—all the love and sadness and cynicism that can be mustered torturously packed into a single narrative. *Cordyceps* is a symbol for the natural world reclaiming dominance over the artificial one.[11] Humans have built empires on asphalt and steel, but nature is always patient, biding its time before sprouting through every crack in the pavement, eventually toppling massive skyscrapers and reducing the monuments of civilization to moss-covered relics. Democracy? Capitalism? Dare we say *religion* or even *objective morality* itself? Like flesh infected by *Cordyceps*, our systems and certainties begin to decay and suddenly give way to the natural world. The question we can ask ourselves at this point, in such a post-*Cordyceps* reality, is not whether good or evil will triumph, but whether such categories even matter.

## Apocalyptic Literature as a Human Mirror

It is a crucial tenet within the tradition of apocalyptic storytelling to use the end of the world, not to predict the future, but to hold a mirror to the present.[12] The *Epic of Gilgamesh*, with its Genesis-esque flood narrative, reflects ancient Mesopotamian anxieties about death and divine impulse. The Book of Revelation—contrary to what the "Left Behind" theologians will erroneously tell you—cautions against the machine of the Roman Empire, but cloaks itself in allegory and blood-red beasts (for historically obvious reasons). Margaret Atwood's *The Handmaid's Tale* imagines a theocratic dystopia built on today's very real misogynistic systems of power. Each of these texts pull back the curtain on human nature and uncover what has always been present—the systemic rot of racism, bigotry, homophobia, misogyny, xenophobia, oligarchy, and greed that structure our "great" societies.

*The Last of Us* does this, too, but whereas Revelation offers judgment and the hope of eschatological redemption, our story offers no such ending to the human drama. There is no new heaven, no new earth.[13] Only a planet ruined (that is, ruined for *us*). And while *The Handmaid's Tale* rages against a system that still functions, *The Last of Us* presents a world in which systems have failed entirely. There is no moral resolution here, and, unlike what one of my heroes, Dr. Martin Luther King once said, no arc that bends toward justice.[14] On the surface, there is only survival. Feral, untamed survival.

## The Collapse of Moral Frameworks

In the world prior to the outbreak, humanity operates within its structures. For better or worse, we have governments, laws, and religions. Ethics are scaffolded into our institutions, propped up by a shared belief in the system and the consequences so often arbitrarily put into place. When these systems collapse, however, so too does our moral compass. The survivors of the outbreak don't debate theology, philosophy, or metaphysics from their seminarian ivory towers, nor do they get into Twitter beefs with rightwing incels on the internet. They trade bullets and weed for penicillin and clean socks.

In this moral vacuum, the only thing that can emerge is a brutal yet pragmatic ethic where morality becomes a function of necessity. *Would it be wrong to kill a man if it meant feeding your starving family?* Maybe, but if the lives of our own families were on the line, I doubt any of us would have much choice. *How about pulling the trigger on another family just because your boss told you to?* That would be a whole other matter, but every decision in this cruel world seems to fall on some kind of spectrum of moral ambiguity.

Nevertheless, few moments capture humanity's collapse as vividly as the death of Sarah in the opening moments of the game. Joel, a father desperate to protect his teenage daughter, is refused aid by the very institutions humanity's so-called "social contract" demands we trust implicitly. A United States soldier—*someone who has sworn to protect the citizens of the country they claim to love*—shoots a wounded child in her father's arms. Instantly, the illusion of safety, of goodness, of any shared moral fabric, shreds like old worn cloth. Joel's "baby girl" dies, not because of *Cordyceps*, but because of fear. Because of bureaucracy. Because when it's the end of the world as we know it, we *don't* feel fine. We panic. And in our panic, the innocent are always the first to be sacrificed.

That is why for years I have said that the end of the world will not come about like fire from heaven. It will come from within. The four riders of the apocalypse of John, incidentally, represent what *we* do to ourselves. To put it this way: they are more anthropological than theological.[15] And so, if we are being brutally honest, the scary monsters in this story are not the infected—though they *are* frightening—the scary monsters are *us*. We are the ones who lose meaning at the end of the world as circumstances force us to ask who we are, and perhaps more poignantly, who we have been all along. Do we merely follow orders? Do we choose whom to save and whom to kill? When meaning is shaken from its foundation, what takes its place?

## SURVIVAL AS THE NEW LAW

"To survive it is often necessary to fight and to fight you have to dirty yourself."[16]

### — GEORGE ORWELL

When the world ends, rules get erased. Every statute, every moral commandment, every "thou shalt not" etched into the foundations of a so-called civilized society is reduced to the smudged remnants of a memory. There are no more laws to break when the law itself no longer exists, nor a constitution to uphold when the ink has long since faded from the pages. In *The Last of Us*, survival becomes law. Joel admits as much immediately after being confronted on moral grounds by Tess in the capitol building in Boston: "Tess, we are survivors!"[17]

Are Tess and Joel "shitty people," as *she* states? Or are they just doing what they can to survive, as Joel retorts? Gone is the social contract, so how can anyone really say for sure? That invisible handshake we have all agreed to, the one that promises we will be decent to each other so long as there are schools to attend, jobs to work, and police and fire stations to call when shit goes sideways, is gone. In its place? Survival—*instinct, self-preservation,* and *desperation*. This is the new moral trinity.

The series doesn't flinch in showing how fast that shift can happen. Soldiers shoot children, not because they necessarily want to, but because someone with a radio tells them to. And in living this way, the calculus of safety includes the cold-blooded murder of the innocent. *Because a child might be infected, and one infected person can doom everyone.* Due to such savage instincts, insurgents end up revolting against tyranny, but their rebellion soon mutates into terror. Fireflies plant bombs in crowded streets. FEDRA agents torture in dark rooms. No one's hands are clean. And the more they fight for freedom, the more the freedom itself becomes stained by the means they use to get it.

But perhaps the most worrying figures are not the soldiers or the revolutionaries. It's the everyday survivors we see in the mirror reflecting ourselves back to us—the ones who steal to feed their siblings, lie to keep the peace, and kill to protect someone they love. The ones who barter not just with goods, but with trust. These are the people *we* might become. Not villains, not heroes, just desperate humans doing whatever the moment demands. In this collapsed world, there are no yellow lines, no fences, no warning signs. The guardrails we have always relied on—churches, schools, governments, hospitals—have rusted away or been blown to bits.

Imagining what you would do, considering such a world-changing event, is a cruel but important thought experiment: Who would *you* become if there were no more socially accepted rules? If there was no one left to arrest you, no God to judge you, no community to shame you, what actions would *you* justify? Would you still be *you*? Or would you become something else? Something feral, something efficient, something necessary for survival?

*The Last of Us* refuses to answer these questions. Instead, it hands us a mirror and dares us to be the ones who gaze into it, challenging us to see that moral clarity might just be a product of comfort, not character. But when comfort is gone, what is left to remain other than moral compromise?

## The Death of the Manichean Good Guy

While we'll explore these ideas in greater depth in chapter 5, it's worth noting here that if the apocalypse kills anything faster than civility, it's the myth of the Manichean "good guy." That old black-and-white heroism we're so used to—the lone gunslinger, the noble protector, the guy who shoots straight and sleeps soundly—is dead and buried somewhere between Austin and Salt Lake City.

Joel Miller is our case study here. A father turned smuggler turned guardian, he is, for all intents and purposes, not a good man. To use Tess' word: *shitty*. But he's not a reductively bad man either. He's simply a father, broken by the unimaginable, who learns to adapt and survive. And in the moral entropy of this new world, adaptation is the only virtue that matters to many of the survivors. He lies, he kills, he betrays, but he also loves. He also protects. He also remembers how to feel, even if only in glimpses. And *that*, more than righteousness or principle, is what makes him the very real human many of us have grown to love.

Tess, Joel's partner in this brutal game of survival, puts it plainly: "We are shitty people, Joel. It's been that way for a long time."[18] She doesn't say it in shame or anger. It's not a confession. It's simply the truth as *she* sees it. Tess and Joel are not villains. And they're certainly not saints. They are just people trying to make it through another shitty day in a shitty world that refuses to reward goodness, gives less than a shit about virtue, and never forgives mistakes.

In another universe—one where his beloved daughter doesn't die in his arms—Joel might have remained a contractor, honed his skills in painting or songwriting, or gotten into gardening or reading Tolkien. In *this* world, however, he's forced to become a killer who shoots an accomplished physician in cold blood to save a girl who never asked to be saved. And somehow, we understand and empathize with such a decision. Somehow, we don't look away, with many of us unflinchingly pulling the trigger as if we never had a choice. That's the power of this story (and indeed all good apocalypses). It breaks down our sense of right and wrong not by challenging it with argument, but by suffocating it with context. *If you are a father, what would you do if your "baby girl" was about to be killed in the name of science and medicine?*

All told, traditional storytelling offers up a hero that goes on a journey, faces obstacles, defeats evil, and comes home transformed.[19] The reason so many of us love and are repulsed by *The Last of Us* is that it spits on such a formula and forces us to adapt. Joel doesn't return home to Texas. Ellie doesn't get closure in Seattle or Santa Barbara. Evil isn't defeated; it just evolves. And transformation? It happens, but not always in the direction we'd like. Sometimes the hero becomes a liar. Sometimes the savior becomes the threat. Sometimes the only arc is survival.

Survival is not heroic, however. Don't mistake me here. It is gritty. It is selfish. It can be cruel. But in the true spirit of *The Last of Us*, survival also cannot be the end-all-be-all, lest we end up surviving for something that is not worth living for.

## MEANING IN THE ASHES

> "My mission in life is not merely to survive, but to thrive; and to do so with some passion, some compassion, some humor, and some style."[20]
>
> — MAYA ANGELOU

Survival is just the beginning of the story, but it is certainly not the end. In *The Last of Us*, staying alive is the lowest bar, not the highest calling. The real struggle lies in what comes after—the *why*, not the *how*. This is not a story about rebuilding civilization; it's about clawing meaning from the rubble in whatever way possible. After all, human beings are nothing if not meaning-making "machines," even if we find ourselves thrust into the end of the world, devoid of such meaning.

"Endure and survive," Ellie reads aloud from her *Savage Starlight* comic. This phrase is half a joke and half a prayer. As we find out from her conversations with Sam, it's not clear whether she believes it. But in a world where hope is dangerous, maybe disbelief is safer. Maybe the people who laugh at mantras are the ones most desperate to believe them.

And yet, every faction in this desperate world tries to create meaning from *something*. They try to turn pain into purpose. FEDRA doubles down on control, curfews, and concrete borders. Power is their gospel, but it is *not* good news.[21] The Fireflies chase salvation, but their holy text is etched in child sacrifice. "This is our future. Think of all the lives we'll save," says Dr. Anderson just before Joel splatters his brains all over the hospital floor. How many countless sacrificial religions have said the same exact thing just before tossing a virgin into a volcano?

The WLF trades ideology for discipline. They are order incarnate: violent, tribal, and insular mimetic doubles of their archnemesis, FEDRA. Like FEDRA, their "prayers" are shouted through megaphones from their thrones of metal and wheels. Meanwhile, the Seraphites renounce modernity and craft their religion from whispers and blood, worshipping a prophet carved into cracked and caving walls and echoed in sycophantic chants. Far from the prophet's original intent, they gut others in silence. Their devotion is pure and their methods purifying. "Feel her love," they say before the knife drops.

But these institutions crumble under the weight of their own contradictions. FEDRA rots from the inside, the Fireflies flicker out, the WLF implodes from the underpinnings of its own hypocrisy. And the Seraphites? Like so many of our religions, they are holy until their holiness turns to divinely ordained evil. No one is immune to the collapse, but no one is wholly guilty for it either.

So, the question is again posed: Where can *meaning* be found in an apocalypse?

For Joel, meaning is simple. *Ellie*. After all he's been through—first with the loss of Sarah, and then with her near surrogate—everything comes down to Ellie. After twenty years and against his every survivalist impulse, she becomes the axis around which Joel's world begins to turn. Not because she is *the* cure; she is simply *his* cure. A second chance at fatherhood. A reason not to pull the trigger whilst the gun is turned on himself. "You have no idea what loss is,"[22] he says, and when he says it, we believe him.

But meaning for Ellie isn't so neat. She had once thought she was born to save the world, but when Joel steals that possibility from her, he doesn't just rob her of her perceived life's purpose, he replaces it with a lie. "Swear to me... that everything you said about the Fireflies is true," she pleads.

"I swear."

"Okay."[23]

It is the softest betrayal, and it echoes forever, causing Ellie's compass to spin wildly. She becomes a rickety boat without a rudder, drifting on a sea of pure vengeance. Like Lamech from the Book of Genesis, revenge is dished out "seventy times seven,"[24] and we all better pray for the motherfucker who gets in Ellie's way. Joel ends up dead, and with his death, so is the chance for her full reconciliation with him. Meaning is buried just outside Jackson's dirt, and Ellie digs through bodies upon bodies to find it again. But vengeance, like heroin mainlined into hardened veins, gives nothing back but death. It is a black hole that swallows all light whole, never flinching for even a second.

Abby mirrors Ellie, but in reverse. Her path to meaning begins in revenge: Joel kills her father, who is her backbone, so years later she returns the favor on a particularly snowy day in Wyoming. However, somewhere in the wreckage of the aftermath, she encounters a Seraphite boy named Lev. And through her relationship with this "child of the enemy," something in Abby shifts. Her path becomes one of protection rather than punishment. Redemption doesn't come in glory; it comes in the quiet recesses of her heart, soul, and mind as she walks away from her final confrontation with Ellie carrying nothing but scars[25] and a second chance.

Please do not misunderstand me, however. None of these complex and contradictory characters are meant to be moral exemplars. Joel is a liar. Ellie is a killer. Abby is a war criminal with a heart. But each of them is grasping at meaning with shaky hands. Not because meaning is noble, but because it is necessary. Without it, we are all are just ghosts with pulses.

God, in this world, seems either dead or disinterested. There are no burning bushes, no loaves, no fishes. Just mold and spores and silence. The Seraphites build a faith out of fragments, no doubt, but their sacrificial rituals are scaffolding for survival, not communion with the divine. Religion is rebar in their crumbling society. And the Fireflies? They crown Ellie the messiah and offer her up on the altar of utilitarianism.[26] Save the many. Sacrifice the one. (I wonder what René Girard would say about this!)

And yet, still they search. For answers. For guidance. For meaning amidst an apocalypse.

"When you're lost in the darkness, look for the light." The slogan lingers like graffiti on the soul. But in this context, it is a bitter proverb, isn't it? Because the darkness is not just outside. It's *in* them. *In* us. As Aleksandr Solzhenitsyn once poignantly wrote, "The line separating good and evil passes not through states, nor between classes, nor between political parties either—but right through every human heart—and through all human hearts."[27]

The light, then, when it comes, is flickering and small. A pun in a pun book. A dinosaur museum in the woods. A guitar string gently plucking the chords to "Take on Me" in the aftermath of slaughter. These fleeting moments of light in the dark are not triumphs. They are respites. A breath between horrors.

And yet, *they matter*.

Because *we* matter.

The existential truth of the matter is the search for meaning might be futile, but it's all we have. When the world ends, so do many of the myths we have constructed to explain it. *The Last of Us* offers no divine blueprint and no grand moral arc. Just people clinging to love, purpose, and memory, all stumbling through the darkness with nothing but a flicker of light in their hands. And sometimes, yes, that flicker is a monstrous lie. But even a lie can warm you for a while. Even a myth can get you through the night and, as J.R.R. Tolkien once put it, "shakily guide us toward the true harbor."[28]

Maybe that's the point. Maybe meaning doesn't need to be eternal to be real. Maybe the light doesn't have to be blinding to be beautiful. In the shattered world of *The Last of Us*, goodness survives in fragments: a shared laugh, a hand extended, a song strummed for someone you love. These moments may not save the world, but they save something far more intimate. They save our humanity.

So, we endure. We survive. We love. Not because the world is good, but because meaning is. And that, in the end, might just be enough light needed for us to go on amidst an apocalypse.

## 2

# ENDURE AND SURVIVE

*The Nature of Suffering and Loss*

*"You're gonna be okay, baby. Stay with me. I'm gonna pick you up. I know, baby, I know... Sarah... Baby? Don't do this to me, baby. Don't do this to me, baby girl. Come on."*[1]

— JOEL MILLER

For better or for worse, religion has always tried to explain the nature of suffering. And while on the surface this seems like a noble cause, every elucidation falls just short (though some explanations *are* better than others). The Buddhist tradition builds an entire philosophical framework on suffering, rightly placing it at the very center of human experience. Life is suffering, says the First Noble Truth. The cause is desire. The solution? Let go. But who among us actually knows how to let go of the desire to let go, not to mention let go of love, of memory, of the hope that meaning can yet be found on the other side of trauma? Liberation from desire sounds nice on paper until you are holding the body of someone you love who, not ten minutes prior, was perfectly healthy and functioning.

Christian theology—something I am (fortunately or unfortunately) *very* familiar with[2]—runs the full spectrum, from the tender co-suffering God of Jürgen Moltmann to the cold, capricious Calvinist deity who predestines your eternal agony and calls it just. Moltmann paints an image of a God on a cross, crying out alongside us, while John Piper, Paul Washer, and too many of my past youth group friends give us a white, male, divine chess master who, for reasons known only to himself, dictates everything and calls the carnage holy. (I have often described this morally and semantically nihilistic God as Janus-faced, as he reminds us of the Roman deity depicted as having two opposing faces.[3])

Then there's Judaism, where the conversation itself *is* the theology. In the poems of Job, in the lamenting of the Psalms, in the heated arguments of rabbis across the ages, we see a tradition unafraid to put God on trial.[4] Is suffering a punishment for sin? A side effect of free will or the *yetzer hara*?[5] A mystery to be held, not solved? It depends on who you ask.

The open and relational theologians—folks like Thomas Jay Oord, Mark Karris, and Chad Bahl—go one step further and say God *can't* stop suffering.[6] Not *won't*. *Can't*. Because true love does *not* control; it only invites and works alongside humans in achieving respite and relief. This God is always calling, never coercing, always present but never imposing. And sure, such a theodicy is a compelling vision, one much more coherent than the dictatorial God who finds glory in our demise. But as we have learned from *The Last of Us*, a strong case can be made that love in fact *can* and *should* coerce when necessary—that is why we would all shove Ellie out of the way of a charging bloater, or wish Tommy had arrived five seconds earlier so that the only relevant bullet discharged on Outbreak Day is the one put in that sycophantic soldier's head.

All told, in *The Last of Us*, we don't get a doctrine. We don't get a theory of pain. Instead, what we get is context. Bloody, messy context. Here, in *this* story, there is no divine logic to the *Cordyceps* outbreak, no religious prophet sees it coming,[7] and certainly no messiah arrives to fix it (though many false messiahs try).[8] And as such, perhaps there is no meaning to the problem of suffering. Or, better yet, maybe that there is no overt meaning *is* the meaning, and all we can do is endure alongside those we love.

## SUFFERING AS THE NARRATIVE ENGINE

"There will always be suffering. But we must not suffer over the suffering."

— **ALAN WATTS**, *Out of Your Mind*

In many of our favorite stories—especially the ones more easily digested by our younger selves—suffering functions merely as a footnote. An obstacle. A necessary evil that must be endured en route to a redemptive conclusion that makes us feel all warm and fuzzy inside. The loss of Obi-Wan Kenobi forces Luke Skywalker to mature into the Jedi he is destined to become.[9] The betrayal of Mother Gothel teaches Rapunzel to distrust any tower erected by those who do not have our best interests in mind, which eventually leads to her liberation. The exile, the illness, the death. All these obstacles are permitted—or worse, ordained by Piper's God of pure caprice—to teach us something profound about life and love and the moral arc of the universe.

But *The Last of Us* offers no such consolation. There is no divine thread running through its violence to pull us toward some cosmic catharsis. As we mentioned in the previous chapter, God seems nowhere to be found in this universe, so there fails to be any grand *telos* awaiting those who manage to endure the bloodshed. Suffering is not a gateway to something better. Instead, it is the entire architecture of the story. Put this way: in *The Last of Us*, suffering is not a bump in the road; it *is* the road.

The first couple minutes of *Part I*—before we can even settle into the gameplay mechanics—make this horrifyingly clear. We meet Sarah, who, like my own daughter of nearly the same age, is witty, kind, clever, and blonde.

She gives her dad a watch for his birthday, cracking a joke about how she had to sell "hardcore drugs" to pay for it.[10] Then, in what seems like a flash (but only after being endeared to Joel's "baby girl"), we hear the music swell, see the darkness fall, and witness her state-sanctioned execution. And not because she does anything wrong, but because bureaucratic protocol demands it. Joel cradles Sarah's body in his arms, his cries of agony being he first prayer we hear, and like all prayers in this universe, they go unanswered.

This is not simply the prologue to the story. It's a thesis informing us that there are no safe zones here, and no narrative armor to be worn. In this godless universe, there is no divine intervention to protect the innocent. Here, death is always around the corner, and we get a glimpse of that before we even get to the game's main narrative.

## No One Is Immune, Especially Not Ellie

Everyone in this story carries trauma like a second skin. Tess knows she is dying the moment she's bitten and chooses to go out, guns blazing, for the sole purpose of buying Joel and Ellie precious time. It is not a noble sacrifice, but a bitter compromise.

Bill's story, on the other hand, is one of loss rather than true companionship.[11] When we find his partner Frank, he is already dead, killed in the end not by the infected, but by hopelessness and despair. Unless it is just his sick sense of humor—and perhaps it is, we can never know for sure—his suicide note is filled with loathing for Bill, who, it seems, failed to love him in the way he needed to be loved. What we're left with is not a testament to romantic endurance in the face of ruin, but the cruel reality that sometimes, contrary to what The Beatles sang, love is *not* all you need.

Henry and Sam give us perhaps the most harrowing example of what trauma does when stacked atop the fragile scaffolding of a fool's hope. Sam is bitten. Henry kills him to spare Ellie from his rage. Then, unable to live with what he's done, Henry takes his own life before Joel or Ellie can stop him.

Even Marlene—one of the last remaining people with a shred of idealism—meets her end with a bullet in her gut at the bloody hands of Joel. This happens, not because she is evil incarnate, but because she tries to do what human beings have done since the dawn of our existence: sacrifice the one to save the many. It's a tale as old as time.[12]

Which brings us all the way back to Joel. His suffering is like that of countless people before him. His daughter dies, his faith dies, his ability to believe in anything resembling *the good* dies. But unlike the biblical character Job, he doesn't receive restored fortunes. He doesn't come out of the ashes with a renewed sense of God's goodness. For twenty years, he grows to become increasingly harsher, hardened, and bitterly cold.

And yet, ironically, it's through suffering that Joel begins to feel again. Slowly. Reluctantly. Against nearly every fiber in his body. Not because it makes him a better person—in one way, he and Tess will always be "shitty people"[13]—but because Ellie worms her way into the hole Sarah has left behind. Joel is not healed by Ellie's presence; he is haunted by it, terrified that if he gets too close, *it* could happen again.

Then he makes the "mistake" of loving her anyway.

But even Joel's development arc is not presented as redemptive. There is no moment where Ellie forgives him and the heavens part with raucous applause. Instead, their story ends with a lie that is never fully dealt with—a young girl robbed of her perceived meaning by a man desperate to preserve his. "Swear to me," she says. "Swear to me that everything you said about the Fireflies is true."

"I swear," he lies.

"Okay," she sighs.[14]

As we will discover in chapter 8, the way she utters this one word tells us everything. There is no true closure here, only tension. Only suffering transformed, not resolved.

This, I believe, is one thing that makes *The Last of Us* more honest than most fiction: it doesn't pretend that pain perfects us. It doesn't suggest that grief inevitably gives birth to wisdom. Sometimes, it just leaves scars and calcifies the heart. Sometimes, it turns us into something less than we were, not because we're weak, but because we are humans—fragile, grief-stricken, breakable humans.

## THE THEODICY OF THE LAST OF US

If there *is* a theodicy in *The Last of Us*, then, it is not a message that can be proclaimed from the pulpits of prosperity preachers like Joel Osteen or Kenneth Copeland. And unlike the countless denominations who present their message with eschatological certainty and a promise of a heavenly prize for those who suffer well, this story bludgeons us across the head with only a question of how much we can endure after the world ends. In other words, a theology of silence that can only be found in the aftermath of chaos. Anything past that is choked out by the sobs of a father cradling his dead daughter. Or, in Abby's case, a daughter mourning the gruesome killing of her dad. The theodicy—again, if we dare to even call it that—is not a theory of why we suffer but the quiet acknowledgment that, in the face of suffering, we are never going to be given a satisfactory answer. We are only given each other, and sometimes not even that.

Whereas traditional theology demands a reason—some cause, some divine calculus that ensures all this pain must *mean* something—*The Last of Us* offers only a blank page and a hell of a bloodstain. If anything, it dares to suggest what few Christian theologians are willing to admit: perhaps there is no meaning behind our pain, and if there is, it is not owed to us. Simone Weil once wrote, "The extreme greatness of Christianity lies in the fact that it does not seek a supernatural cure for suffering, but a supernatural use for it."[15] But even Weil, in all her deep wisdom and mysticism, seeks some function or salvific purpose behind our agony. *The Last of Us* offers no such consolation. It only asks: *What the fuck do we do now?*

Compare this with David, the cannibalistic preacher and perhaps the most theologically perverse character in the franchise. When Ellie is captured by his group in *Part I*, he attempts to soothe her by saying, "It was God's will...

everything happens for a reason."[16] On its face, and depending upon your upbringing, this line sounds benign and perhaps even comforting. We've heard such sentiment preached from pulpits, whispered in hospital waiting rooms, broadcasted on countless Instagram reels, blurted anytime someone doesn't know what else to say during unexplainable tragedy. But here, from the mouth of a predator, it is exposed for what it truly is: a tool of colonization and control. David's words are the epitome of the spiritualization of abuse, a justification for perverted horror masquerading as saintly faith.

David is not merely a monster. He is a doctrinal nightmare come to life, the incarnate consequence of a theology that defines goodness as whatever God does, no matter how despotic or horrific. In that sense, he is Calvinism in the flesh, a man who believes that unequivocal power equals righteousness. "If God does it, it *must* be good," he would coldly say to Plato,[17] even if it looks like hell to the rest of us. This is the same logic that fuels John Piper's claim that, "it's right for God to slaughter women and children anytime he pleases."[18] Why? Because—and forgive me for the absurd tautology—God is God. But this is nothing more than divine voluntarism unmasked, a pathetic excuse for a theodicy, built not on love, but on power and dominance.

*The Last of Us* vomits this out like cafeteria slop three days spoiled. And rightfully so. Ellie does not find peace through surrender to some preordained divine plan, nor does she accept that what happens to her is for her growth or sanctification. She survives by butchering David in the most brutal way imaginable. Repeatedly. Desperately. Ironically, given that he had previously threatened to, and I quote, "chop her up into little bits"—a hell of a thing to say to a fourteen-year-old girl. However, she rejects his worldview, and, by extension, that of every narcissist who has ever tried to cover atrocity with the shambolic perfume of power and providence.

The deafening theological silence found in the game is not empty, though, nor does it present a purely nihilistic vision of the universe. In fact, its gospel message is quite loaded. It says what countless traumatized people have come to understand: that no one is coming to save you, that the reasons given for your pain are often just as violent as the pain itself, and that the only thing worse than meaningless suffering is the attempt to spiritualize it. And in this void (of bad theology), there you will find its beauty. That to be human is to be present. With ourselves. With others. With the tactile and tragic and terrible and transcendent that permeates the totality of everything around us. It's not a theological system, per se, but a quiet refusal to "go gentle into that good night."[19] It's Ellie staying with Joel after he's been impaled. It's Dina making a home for Ellie in Jackson. It's Abby choosing to surrender to Ellie on the beach. It's Lev whispering prayers even when he doesn't know who, if anyone, is listening. It's the strum of the guitar, the desperate corniness of the pun book, the small acts of grace between people who have nothing to gain by giving it.

Again, there may be no God in this story, but there is Love. And that is indeed *good news*.

If we borrow from Dietrich Bonhoeffer, whose *Letters and Papers from Prison* attempted to articulate a "religionless Christianity," we might say that *The Last of Us* is a gospel for a world where God is not coming, but where we still must act as if love is sacred. "God lets himself be pushed out of the world on to the cross," Bonhoeffer writes. "He is weak and powerless in the world, and that is precisely the way, the only way, in which he is with us and helps us."[20] Except in *The Last of Us*, there is no cross and no resurrection. Only presence. A hand on a shoulder. A meal shared. Even a crass and pornographic joke between a teenage girl and her father-figure.

So, let me again reiterate: in *The Last of Us*, the absence of a theodicy then becomes its own kind of theodicy. Not an explanation for suffering, but a positioning and a posture within it.

The world is broken, no doubt. And we can be confident that there is no divine judge coming to make it right. No terrifying final boss fight against the Rat King will cleanse it of its rot. The best we can do is sit in the ashes with each other, hold space for the pain, and choose, again and again, to *not* walk away. That is the gospel of *The Last of Us*, and it may be the only good news we have in this fucked-up and decaying world.

## 3

# LOOK FOR THE LIGHT

*Finding Love in a Loveless World*

> "There are a million ways we should've died before today, and a million ways we can die before tomorrow. But we fight... for every second we get to spend with each other."[1]
>
> — **RILEY ABEL**

If *The Last of Us* has anything like a traditional salvation story, it is not rooted in miracles or messianic deliverance. Nobody gets caught up by the Holy Spirit, nor do they get healed or raised from the dead like Lazarus. And, contrary to what the Seraphites would say, there are no readily-available prophets. There are just broken people clinging to each other in a broken world, daring against all odds to continue giving a shit.

Love, then, never descends to this world from above or adorned with angel's wings. Instead, it comes to us delivered by a busted-ass '91 Chevy S10 crew cab that can barely make it up a hill. It's loud, rusty, and impossible to ignore. This love doesn't always save. How could it? But it does refuse to leave. As we've explored already, it is the act of pure presence amidst an apocalypse, arms linked by two people ready to face hell head-on.

If chapter 2 of this book asked what we do with our pain, this chapter asks what we do with our hearts. This is not the neat, sanitized kind of lovey-dovey heart stuff, either. This is a kind of love that bleeds real human blood. The kind that forces impossible decisions by imperfect people. The kind that absolutely ruins every single one of our presuppositions about what we thought the world was really like.

In the section that follows, let's start by exploring the love some of our favorite (and not-so-favorite) characters have for each other, and how such love shapes their lives and stories, as messy as they often are.

## LOVE AS THE TIE THAT BINDS

### Joel and Ellie: Love That Protects at All Costs

Let's revisit the moment everything falls apart.

Joel's love for Sarah isn't dramatic like what we might see on TV. It's not even that verbal. He's just a regular dad doing his best, and, to be fair, his efforts probably would earn him a B-minus grade. But who am I to judge? I, too, am just a dad doing his best. Plus, no one expects the world to end on their birthday, so what more could we want from Joel? When Sarah is shot, a father doesn't just lose a child; he loses his tether, his compass, his one good reason for waking up in the morning.

What follows is not grief in the usual sense. There is no funeral, nor a eulogy to reflect on. Just silence. And then twenty years of letting that silence calcify into something hard and impenetrable. Joel becomes a man who survives, not a man who truly lives. Instead, he refuses to love again, refuses to get close to anything except the safety of distance. Because closeness, as Bill makes perfectly clear, ends in ruin. "Once upon a time I had someone I cared about," the rugged survivalist admits. "It was a partner. Somebody I had to look after. And in this world that sort of shit's good for one thing: gettin' ya killed."[2]

Then comes Ellie—not exactly a case of paternal love at first sight. Ellie is a nuisance. A job. "Cargo," as she's unaffectionately referred to. But, she is also a reminder of what Joel is trying to forget. The slow burn, like that of a perfectly rolled Cuban cigar, is inevitable. Somewhere between the puns and the firefights, between winter and spring, between "you're not my daughter"[3] and "baby girl, it's okay,"[4] Joel's walls come down. Not all at once. And only just enough for something like love to crawl through the cracks.

By the time we get to the Firefly hospital, that love has become a matter of survival, only, not hers. *His*. Joel doesn't save Ellie because she's the future of humanity. He saves her because she's *his* future. And in saving her, he damns the rest of the world, if that's even what was at stake. (We'll get into the ethics of *that* moment in a later chapter.)

This is the raw reality of the sort of love depicted in *The Last of Us*: one life, one bond, qualitatively worth more than the rest of the world. Which may not be morally sound, but it is real. It is human. And for Joel—any B-minus or above father, really—it is everything.

## Sam and Henry: Love That Protects, Until It Can't

Then there's the kind of love that tries to protect... *and fails*.

Henry is not a hardened soldier. He is not a killer. He's not, in short, Joel. But he *is* a big brother, and big brothers will do what big brothers gotta do to protect their "little bro." Henry's love for Sam is fierce, desperate, and utterly unprepared for the world they've been born into and trapped by. When Sam is bitten, we see the full weight of love collapse in half a heartbeat. Henry shoots his own brother to save Ellie, and then, just as quickly, turns the gun on himself.

This is the epitome of love without a plan or a safety net, without any semblance of a stable community. And that, too, is part of what *The Last of Us* teaches us: sometimes love is *not* enough. Sometimes it breaks you.

Sometimes the only way to love someone in a world like this is to die beside them and let those who are left behind pick up the pieces.

## Ellie and Dina: Love That Attempts to Heal

Ellie has every reason not to let anyone into her life. Her story is a trail of grief and abandonment. Riley, her first love… gone. Tess… gone. Sam, Henry, and eventually Joel and Jesse… gone, gone, gone, and fucking gone. And then, after all the carnage of the open road, Dina arrives. Not with a solution, not with a map out of the trauma, but with warmth (an important quality in a snowy place like Jackson). Dina arrives with curiosity, the audacity to joke, to flirt, to stay beside Ellie when we all damn well know Ellie has little to give in return.

There's something quietly radical about the way Dina loves Ellie. She doesn't try to fix her by psychoanalyzing or spiritualizing Ellie's trauma. Dina simply offers herself moment by moment. And for a while, that's enough. They build something in Jackson that almost looks like stability. They slow down. They exhale. They name their baby JJ. There are string lights and records and a little slice of pretend-normal carved into the farmland.

But normal doesn't last in this world if trauma is not properly addressed.

Ellie's love for Joel—and the grief that remains tangled in it—starts to gnaw at the edges of what she and Dina have built. Revenge becomes a siren song. And love, instead of being the thing that anchors Ellie, drives a stake between her and the life in front of her. When Dina asks her to stay, Ellie admits, "I can't."[5] And she means it. There is no choice from where she stands.

Of course, Ellie doesn't leave to kill Abby because she fails to care, but because she cares too much. She needs Joel's death to mean something because he's the one who took such meaning away from her. She's willing to risk everything for that, even the one good thing that has come out of her years of trauma.

After ending her pursuit of retribution, Ellie returns to the farmhouse and finds it empty. Are any of us surprised? Can we really blame Dina? She waited. She held on as long as she could. But sometimes, love means walking away before it destroys you, too. I think Ellie would agree with us that Dina deserves such freedom.

And still, we believe that Ellie loves Dina. Deeply. As it stands, she just doesn't know how to hold love and grief at the same time. Or, perhaps Ellie's final encounter on the beach with Abby—especially her ability to finally let go of her vengeance—is the catalyst for her healing, for her to finally accept the full spectrum of the human experience.

## Abby and Lev: Love That Transcends

If Ellie and Dina show us how love can be fractured by vengeance, Abby and Lev show us something closer to its redemption.

Abby doesn't start off as someone particularly open to love. Her world is shaped by loss—the loss of her father, the loss of her moral clarity, the loss of her place in the world after Joel's death shatters what little righteousness she thought she had. Her love, at first, is entirely retrospective. It's devoted to a ghost that haunts her day and night, pushing her to commit one of the most brutal acts in the game.

But then she meets Lev.

Lev is everything Abby isn't: hopeful and curious. He's still unbroken in the ways that matter. And when Abby chooses to protect him, we see something in her start to shift. She doesn't save him to redeem herself. She saves him because he's *worth* saving. Period. Because somewhere along the line, she remembers what it means to care about someone who doesn't owe you anything.

Lev, too, brings his own weight to the relationship. He's lost his sister, his home, his mother. His religion has turned on him—"heretic" is what he has become. And yet, he doesn't give in to bitterness. He doesn't close off. He still has hope and remains curious to the end.

Together, Abby and Lev become something like family, and not the kind forged by blood, but the kind forged by choice and circumstance. And that, in the world of *The Last of Us*, might be the most powerful kind of love there is.

When they drive their rickety boat into the unknown together at the end of the game, it's not triumphant. It is, however, hopeful. Their ending—which, if they both survive, should really be seen as their beginning—is forged from the ashes of loss, but it creates a bond more unbreakable than anything either have ever known.

## THE LAST OF US AND THE PHILOSOPHY OF LOVE

*"Love is giving someone the power to destroy you and trusting them not to use it."*

### — UNKNOWN

By the time we reach the final cutscenes of *Part II*, we realize what the game has been doing all along. It wasn't preparing us to make the right choices. It wasn't even preparing us to live with the wrong ones. It was training us to understand the unbearable weight of giving a shit. Of caring. Of *loving*. Not in the passive, background sense. Not the way we care about our favorite football team—the *mostly* unbearable and insufferable Tottenham Hotspur for me[6]—or the way we hope our preferred rapper wins album of the year. But in the guttural, blood-and-guts-on-the-floor kind of way that redefines what we're willing to endure, and more importantly, who we're willing to become.

Love, in this world, is not a gift, not a miracle, and not even necessarily "good" in the Manichean sense. In all truthfulness, it is a *burden*. It is a weight people carry into every impossible choice, and it's the one thing no one is ever quite ready for. Because in the world of *The Last of Us*, love doesn't arrive neatly packaged in a sacred text with a verse about God *being* love.[7] It doesn't show up as a noble calling or a moral compass. It shows up as a burning house you still run into, as a Taylor guitar you wish you could still play, as the moment your hand hesitates before delivering the kill shot because *they* remind you of *him* or *her* or *someone you lost and never stopped loving*. In *The Last of Us*, love is inconvenient and yet somehow still vitally crucial to the fabric of its universe.

Joel's love for Ellie is one of the most emotionally complex portrayals of paternal affection in modern storytelling. It's also one of the most morally troubling. He doesn't save her from the hospital in Salt Lake City because it's the right answer to the Trolley Problem.[8] He doesn't save her because it's what she would've wanted (she repeatedly says as much). He saves her because he *can't* lose her. Not again. Not like Sarah. Love, here, is not about consent or justice or the greater good; it's about the sheer inability to live through that kind of loss a second time. And in such a refusal, Joel kills. He lies. He ends the last fragile hope humanity has (assuming the Fireflies are the messianic figures we know, deep down, they aren't). Because his love has nothing left to give the world. He only has something left for one person: *Ellie*.

And yet, we still root for him. We still slaughter everyone in that goddamn hospital, perhaps even enjoying every moment of it. Because we get it. We've all imagined what we would do if someone we loved was on the table, sacrificed for the greater good according to a paramilitary group comprised entirely of morally compromised people.

So, is Joel a monster?

Or is he the only one who remembers what it means to be human, to love *unconditionally*?

Then there's Ellie, whose love for Joel warps into something darker than a moonless night the moment he's taken from her. She calls it justice, but really, it's love in mourning, the dark side of the Force, to mix fictional universes. Ellie's journey isn't about closure; it's about preservation. As I've stated already, she needs Joel's death to *mean something*, because if it doesn't, she fears losing *her* meaning. And just as troubling: she may conclude that their love didn't matter.

Abby's story, while less embraced by some fans, is equally rich in what it says about love. Her entire arc begins with a different kind of grief, the grief of discovering her dead father at the hands of someone who loved too much. And in her retaliation, she becomes what she hates. Then Lev appears, and for the first time, love is no longer disoriented. It isn't about revenge. It isn't about ghosts. *It's about someone still alive.* Someone she can still protect. Someone whose future might matter more than her past. Her violence doesn't redeem her, but her love for Lev reorients her toward her true nature.

Lev, in turn, teaches us something quieter, something more resilient. His love is nothing if not consistent, driven by his curiosity and constant questioning. He walks away from a faith that calls him an abomination and a heretic, not with rage, but with resolve. He loses his sister. He forgives Abby. And he carries his story forward, not as a martyr, but as a survivor. That kind of love—resilient, soft-spoken, unyielding—is perhaps the rarest thing in this game, but it is also the most necessary, because it's the most grounded and transcendent.

So, what kind of love survives the end of the world?

*The Last of Us* doesn't give us a clean answer. But it gives us this truth:

> *Love should not be thought of as either good or bad. It is a force. And like all forces, it must be reckoned with. Love can lead to redemption, yes, but it can also leave a scorched earth—or hospital—in its wake. It can heal, but it can destroy. And in the midst of it all, it never leaves anyone unchanged.*

The game doesn't tell you how to feel about any of it. There's no moralizing narrator, no righteous path, no "True Ending" at the culmination of a prescribed, Campbell-esque, hero's journey. Just people loving each other, destroying each other, saving each other, and hopefully never leaving each other. Here, love is not a ladder to a higher truth; it is a weight that pulls characters into the mess of their own humanity. Sometimes it lifts. Sometimes it crushes. But it always reveals *something*.

In the end, *The Last of Us* insists that love is never simple, never clean, and never safe. It is messy and contradictory, as likely to wound as to heal, but it is also the one thing that makes survival more than just breathing. Love doesn't promise happy endings—it rarely promises anything—but it does make the cost of living in such a broken world worth paying. And maybe that's the closest thing we get to an answer: that to love, even when it breaks us, is the only way to remain human at all.

# 4

# SOMETHING TO FIGHT FOR

*Free Will and the Illusion of Choice*

*"It was her. She fought like hell to get here. Maybe it was meant to be..."*[1]

— JOEL MILLER

We love the idea of freedom, don't we? We sing about it in our anthems, bake it into our constitutions, and paste it all over our motivational posters featuring stock photos of soaring bald eagles and purple mountains majesty. In the United States, freedom is our sacred cow—Moses' brother Aaron had a literal calf but ours is symbolic in nature, a worldview that separates us from the "Pinko commies," from the "lower" animals, from whatever we secretly fear we might be.

But here's the uncomfortable question *The Last of Us* asks with an unflinching stare and a bloodstained beard: *Do we really have the type of freedom many claim we have?* Or, more redolent still, *would we even want it if we did?*

Philosophers have been debating this question for millennia. Augustine blamed our broken wills on Original Sin.[2] Kant famously argued for a radical "spontaneity of the will"[3]—this untethered, self-originating capacity to make rationalistic choices. Meanwhile, modern neuroscience humbly, and with devastating evidence,[4] suggests that choices happen in the brain before we're even conscious of them, making our proud declarations of pure, libertarian rational agency feel like little more than narrations over actions already set in motion. German philosopher Arthur Schopenhauer once put it starkly: "Man can do what he wills but he cannot will what he wills."[5] In other words, even our perceived "freedom" rests upon a deeper compulsion, a will that chooses us long before we choose anything ourselves.

Let's be real for a moment, though: we do *not* need Augustine, Kant, Schopenhauer, or a CT scan of the brain to realize something is wrong with the way we in the West typically talk about human volition. Nothing in life comes *tabula rasa*, and deep down, we know human beings are quite complicated. Every "choice" we make seems tied to a thousand invisible strings—trauma, love, fear, mimesis, survival, and so on. Freedom, then, if it exists at all, cannot simply be the ability to choose randomly (the way a cow "chooses" which patch of grass to chew[6]), but the ability to choose *the good*. The problem, most notably, is that *the good* is itself almost always muddy, hidden, or veiled in grief, trauma, and other baggage.

René Girard, the father of mimetic theory, makes such truths painfully obvious. *We are not self-made islands of autonomous desire*, he argues, *we are "interdividuals,"*[7] *fundamentally shaped by the people, communities, gods, and idols we imitate.* Whether we like it or not, our wills are not autonomous and pristine snowflakes gently falling from the heavens; they are weathered tapestries of fears, memories, cultural expectations, prescribed gender roles, and deeply-cut scars stitched together by the countless hands of others, many of whom came and went long before us.

The tragic genius of *The Last of Us* lies in its restraint. As with the problem of suffering, it never offers a theology of free will. It doesn't need to. It simply shows us the truth of our plight: a soldier hesitating for a millisecond before shooting a little girl; a father pulling the trigger without hesitation; a daughter trading her future for vengeance. And in these moments, we see *it*—the illusion of libertarian freedom. The brutal, relentless momentum of life's circumstances. Of pain and love and fear and loss. We *choose*, yes, but the field from which we choose is already prepared, and the options have been narrowed to a point finer than a single fungal spore.

*That* is the real horror for all the "rugged individualists" out there—I'm talking to you, Bill. Not that we sometimes make bad choices, but that we fail to really choose at all. We are carried there, pulled along by tides we barely understand until our hands are bloodied and our hearts broken. Then and only then are we forced to ask: "Was there *truly* ever another way?"

Welcome to the death of the American façade of the Free Individual™, the recognition that *choice* and *will* are two very different things, and to fight for something in this world might be the most human thing we can do, even when it isn't autonomously chosen at all. Which leads us directly, and appropriately, into the mechanics of the story itself—a game that allows you to assume you have agency until it rips it away the moment you need it most.

## THE GAME AS A METAPHOR FOR THE ILLUSION OF FREE WILL

Contemporary video games are obsessed with player choice. They sell it to us like religion, as if *The Sims* didn't come out a quarter-century ago. Massive open worlds. Branching dialogue trees. Moral sliders. Rockstar Games with their reputation meter (as if there is anything that can be done about the imminent death of Arthur Morgan[8]). As if all these digital micro-decisions—stealing a health kit here, sparing a FEDRA soldier there—might one day accumulate into something resembling agency. As if the illusion of choice were enough to satisfy the longing for control.

*The Last of Us* never pretends to care about any of that.

It doesn't hand you a morality meter. It doesn't let you shape Joel into an archetype. It doesn't give you multiple endings or divergent timelines or "press X to forgive." There are no alternate paths. There is only *the* path, and it is paved in blood. You do not get to stop Joel from saving Ellie, no matter how conflicted you are. You do not get to stop Abby from killing Joel, no matter how much you love him. You do not get to stop Ellie from throwing away everything she has remaining, no matter how desperately Dina pleads. The game is *not* interested in *your* permission. Instead, it makes you complicit in everything!

At every pivotal juncture, *The Last of Us* takes the controller from your hands and uses it to point the gun. It forces you into violence, then pries your eyes open before gaslighting you: *Look what you've done, you bastard!* But is Naughty Dog wrong? You *did* do it. You pulled the trigger. I did, too. But did any of us really *choose* to?

Some would call this a flaw or a shortcoming, but it is neither of these things. The game is designed to be this way, because the lack of freedom *is* the message.

Unlike games that wrap you in the warm blanket of consequence-free agency, *The Last of Us* says, "You are going to do horrible things. You are going to watch yourself do them. And then you are going to sit with it." You sit in the hospital hallway, stepping over the corpses of medical professionals allegedly trying to save the world.[9] You sit in the theater, hunting Abby, even as Ellie loses her final connections to humanity. You sit on the beach in Santa Barbara, watching Ellie raise a knife against a woman already starving, already beaten, already broken, and you don't want to press square again.

But you press the button anyway. In fact, you mash it.

Until you don't.

Of course, you don't commit any of this brutality because you necessarily *want* to, but because that's the game. That's the story. That's the inevitability that's been baked into the world and into you.

So, what does this mean?

It means the game is not merely about free will. It *performs* in volition's absence, manipulating the player not to prove a point, but to make you *feel* what the characters feel: trapped by history, by loss, by loyalty, by vengeance.

Joel doesn't save Ellie because he's a monster. He saves her because he *has to*. You don't chase Abby because you're a bad person. You do it because the game makes you. Because the narrative demands it. Because Ellie's grief is now your grief.

It's brilliant. And it's cruel. (And it's also why silly little books like this one get written).

This approach violates the sacred contract of player autonomy and makes you grateful for the betrayal. Because somewhere, deep down, you know that *this is what it actually feels like to live through trauma*. The path narrows. The choices disappear. You don't decide who to become; you just survive the *becoming*.

So yes, you can explore every room, collect every Firefly pendant and comic book, and listen to every optional conversation, but when it matters most, your agency collapses. The outcome is already decided because you are not the author of this story. You are just its witness and accomplice. And that, ironically, might be the most honest depiction of human freedom gaming has ever offered.

## WHEN THE GOOD EMERGES FROM THE ASHES

> "The good is an eternal reality, a transcendental truth that is ultimately identical with the very essence of God."[10]
>
> — **DAVID BENTLEY HART**, *The Experience of God*

This beautiful, tragic, devastating game doesn't just deconstruct libertarian free will, it also refuses the cold comfort of strict, Calvinistic determinism. In case you've misunderstood me to this point, I am not saying that the characters are cogs in a machine, or that they are pawns on a divine chessboard. There is something that *resembles* agency here, but it's murky, painful, and emerges slowly, like early morning light bleeding through boarded-up windows. The characters don't choose freely in the modern Western sense, but neither are they *forever* trapped in the fatalistic currents of trauma. If true freedom is the ability to choose the good, then *The Last of Us* shows us how painfully rare, hard-won, and incomplete that clarity can be.

Bill is the purest case study in the illusion of choice. He insists that he is a free man, "surviving" on his own terms, with explosive booby traps, canned beans and greens, and a hardened ideology about self-reliance. But the moment love touches him—when Frank enters the frame—his walls collapse. Both physical and ideological. He loves Frank, even as he resents needing him. And in the end, his real act of agency isn't hoarding or shooting or isolating; it's choosing to open up to someone who would potentially be forever lost to him. That isn't libertarian free will. That's not clean-cut Kantian autonomy. That's freedom *through* love. That's the good sneaking in through a crack in the concrete.

Abby's journey is different. She, being a melodic echo of Joel but played in a drastically different key, is introduced as a character consumed by revenge. And yet, unlike Joel, she has a chance to step back from total consumption. She meets Lev, and through him, begins to see a different path forward. This isn't some Hallmark moral transformation that transcends in a cringe-worthy come-to-Jesus moment. Abby's arc is a slow, messy evolution—violent, terrifying, and haunted by guilt. But in choosing to risk everything to protect Lev, she finally sees the good. Not abstractly, not philosophically, but concretely, in another human being. In Lev, Abby glimpses something beyond vengeance, beyond survival, beyond her own story.

Then there's Ellie.

Ellie, who has every reason to become a monster and nearly does, loses everything—her father-figure, her lover, her child, her peace—because she cannot stop the forward momentum of revenge. Her will has been hijacked. Her path narrowed. Her options pruned to a single, poisonous branch: *kill*

*Abby*. Finish what Joel started. Or what Joel died for. Or what she *thinks* Joel died for. Something to give her life meaning.

But then, when she finally has a chance to finish Abby, Ellie stops.

It's not clean. It's not redemptive in the classic Hollywood sense. But it's real. For the first time in what feels like forever, Ellie actually makes a *choice*—not out of fear, not out of rage, not because the game demands it—but because something *good* pierces the fog. Maybe it's the image of Joel playing guitar. Maybe it's the innocence of Lev. Maybe it's the exhaustion of carrying her trauma one mile too far. Whatever it is, it gives her clarity. And from that clarity, she chooses the goodness of mercy.

That moment, small as it is, is seismic. Because in that moment, Ellie stops being a puppet of her pain. She lays down her need to win, and in doing so, she wins something else entirely: the flickering possibility of peace.

## THE WISDOM OF GOODNESS

If *The Last of Us* offers any kind of philosophical answer here, it's one forged in the aftermath of devastation. It's not a theology of certainty or victory, but of fragile hope found in the quiet, trembling possibility that amidst the wreckage of our past, we might still find the freedom to choose differently.

This is not the kick-ass freedom peddled by Enlightenment philosophers or America-first politicians. It is not the sort of freedom that ignores trauma, or flattens and whitewashes history, or imagines the will to be some frictionless engine humming along in a perfect vacuum. And it is certainly not the freedom of the libertarian—the myth that we are unshaped, untouched, or ungoverned, floating above the messy materiality of genetics, grief, and generational pain. But neither is this the bleak determinism of Baruch Spinoza or Chrysippus and the Stoics—the idea that we are nothing but dominoes in a causal chain, destined only to fatalistically fall whichever way life tips us. No, the freedom on display in *The Last of Us*—similar to the freedom I wrote about in *The Wisdom of Hobbits*—is something much more humble, much more hopeful. It involves *balance*. It is becoming freer *within* the chaos, not apart from it. It is, to borrow Tolkien's framing, a kind of eucatastrophe: not the undoing of suffering, but the piercing of it by grace. As the Professor once wrote, "The eucatastrophe tale is the true form of fairy-tale... a sudden and miraculous grace: never to be counted on to recur."[11] In that sudden turn, when mercy interrupts the cycle of violence, we find not a denial of darkness, but its transformation.

And yet, as Tolkien suggests, such grace is neither predictable nor permanent. It doesn't *make* us free in the way we might expect; instead, it *helps* us become freer. It is in these moments—when grace offers us a new lens, a chance to shift from vengeance to mercy—that we begin to understand what true freedom looks like.

True freedom is not raw choice. It is clarity. But clarity doesn't come easily. It is hammered out in the flames of consequence. It is whispered in moments of serene mercy. It is shaped in the presence of others—others who wound us, yes, but also through others who call us beyond our wounds.

Sadly, Joel never becomes free. He dies while still trapped in regret. Bill, on the other hand, will probably go on to die grasping at the good but never quite holding it with open hands. Abby finds it only by letting go of vengeance, by tethering her life to Lev. And Ellie—*God bless her*—scratches and claws her way to a moment of lucidity on a beach in California, where she finally lets Abby come up for a breath, thus letting her own soul exhale.

And speaking of God. Here's where some theology comes in. Because again, grace is not God making us "free" in the Cartesian sense; grace is love helping us become *freer*—freer from our compulsions, freer from the inherited scripts that narrow our vision, freer from the endless Lamechian cycle of retaliation.[12] Grace is what turns a melee weapon into a hand extended. Grace is what lets us choose *love*, even if we only get there by going through Dante's nine circles of hell—or, worse yet, a tunnel in Salt Lake City full of runners, clickers, and bloaters.

In a world like ours—a world burning with tribalism, vengeance, and the ghosts of our failures—freedom looks less like autonomy and more like the courage to *see the good and choose it*, even when everything in us wants to look away. That is the grace of *The Last of Us*. Not perfect freedom. But the slow, hard, painful journey of becoming *freer*. Freed not from our trauma, but from its tyranny. Freed not to dominate, but to cooperate. And in that, I think, we catch a eucatastrophic glimpse of something thoroughly divine—freedom found in love.

5

# No Half Measures

*Heroism and the Death of the Good Guy*

*"Guess what, we're shitty people, Joel.
It's been that way for a long time."*[1]

— **TESS SERVOPOULOS**

In *The Wisdom of Hobbits*, I argue that heroism is never simple. It is messy, unpredictable, and often shaped more by mercy and pity than power and might. In Tolkien's world, even the noblest characters are plagued by failure and weakness. Frodo can't bring himself to throw the Ring into Mount Doom. Boromir nearly single-handedly destroys the Fellowship at Amon Hen before redeeming himself in a desperate act of sacrifice. And even Aragorn—the closest thing to a classical Manichean hero—wrestles with doubt, shame, and an overwhelming burden of responsibility. Hence what I wrote back in 2023: "sometimes our heroes are messy and our villains complicated."[2]

In Middle-earth, this complexity is woven into Tolkien's narrative as if knitted by the hand of Ilúvatar himself. There is always room for redemption, always a sliver of hope—even if only "a fool's hope," to borrow Gandalf's words[3]—and always a sense that the characters, no matter how flawed, are still aiming toward the good, even if they fall short.

*The Last of Us* doesn't offer us nearly as much grace.

Whereas Tolkien blurs the line between hero and villain, Druckmann and Naughty Dog tend toward taking an eraser to this distinction. There are no capes, no kingly speeches, no resurrected divine emissaries riding to the rescue on the first light of the fifth day. There's just a man, a girl, a gun, and a world in tatters. And in this world, "heroism" is no longer a meaningful category. In fact, as we will shortly see with the Fireflies, it might be a dangerous one.

Because what *The Last of Us* understands—far more than most modern media—is that in a world stripped of structure, righteousness becomes nearly indistinguishable from selfishness. Joel kills for love, yes, but he also lies for control. Abby seeks justice, but that justice is nothing but Lamechian revenge. Ellie is willing to burn the world down for closure and nearly does. And yet, as disillusioned as we become with our so-called heroes, *The Last of Us* doesn't let us off the hook that easily. *If we can't trust Joel to be the "good guy with a gun," who is left?* we wonder. Surely, someone must carry the torch for this story to "work." Surely, someone must be out there doing the right thing for the right reasons. Enter the Fireflies. The rebels, the idealists, the utilitarians, the motley crew hellbent on saving humanity from the spores and the ashes. Maybe *they* are the righteous heroes. Maybe *they* are what's left of the light.

Indeed, that's what they believe themselves to be. Humanity's heroes. Ragtag resistance fighters. GI Joes for a time such as this. And from a certain angle, if you squint just right and suspend all reason, they *look* the part. Clever name? Hell yeah. Inspiring tagline? I begin this book by quoting it. Leather jackets, fortified bases, and AR-15s? As American as revolution and apple pie.

But let's ask the uncomfortable question: What happens when morally compromised, self-appointed saviors get their hands on "the Ring?" What happens when they gain access to the One Thing That Could Save the

World™? We find out in that now infamous Salt Lake City hospital the minute they grasp at their prize.

Like a trap, they spring, never hesitating for a moment. They don't consult with Ellie, nor do they give two shits about affording Joel a half a second to process a single goddamn thing, let alone even say goodbye. They strap a child down, gather their surgical tools, and prepare to cut into the brain of a living, breathing, conscious fourteen-year-old girl. And they do it without a shred of consent or irony. Just a presumed moral high ground and a physician violating his Hippocratic oath to "do no harm."

Isn't this *exactly* how power works?

In *The Lord of the Rings*, Tolkien's entire moral framework hinges on what people do when they're offered immense power for a seemingly noble end. Galadriel refuses it. Faramir declines it. Frodo begrudgingly carries it, only to come up just short at the Cracks of Doom. But those who *seek* it—Boromir, Saruman, Sauron—they are the ones who become mimetic Melkorian monsters. The Ring doesn't just corrupt the wicked, however. It also corrupts the well-intentioned. Because that's what absolute power does.[4] As the old proverb goes, "the road to hell is paved with good intentions," and boy-oh-boy the Fireflies sure as hell believe themselves to have the best of them.

And yet, here, in our story, the Fireflies aren't evil incarnate. They aren't fascists or warlords. They are scientists, doctors, soldiers, mothers, fathers, sons, daughters, and dear friends, all desperate to make things right. But they—like every archaic, modern, and post-apocalyptic society alike—have convinced themselves that saving the world requires a sacrifice of "the other." For the Fireflies, they have to take away a young girl's choice. Because that's what the Ring whispers. That's what the Ring *always* whispers: "I do not understand all this," says Boromir at the Council of Elrond, "Why should we not think that the Great Ring has come into our hands to serve us in the very hour of need? Wielding it the Free Lords of the Free may surely defeat the Enemy [...] The Men of Gondor are valiant, and they will never submit; but they may be beaten down. Valour needs first strength, and then a weapon.

Let the Ring be your weapon, if it has such power as you say. Take it and go forth to victory!"[5]

Even Marlene—who claims to love Ellie and who promised Anna that she'd protect her—is willing to not only look away but is a cosigner on the entire plan. She tells herself that killing this child is for the greater good. She tells Joel it's what Ellie *would have* wanted, as if asking her, counseling her, and deliberating with her were never an option.

The fucking audacity of this woman...

The tragedy, as it is presented in this narrative at least, is no doubt that Marlene *might* be right. The Fireflies *might* have created a vaccine. Ellie *might* have chosen to give her life. But none of that changes what they actually do, which is rob Ellie of the one thing they claimed to be fighting for: a future. Her future, and the future of all children like her. And in doing so, they reveal what happens when heroism becomes synonymous with control.

Tolkien would have likely viewed the hospital scene as depicting a moral eucatastrophe gone terribly wrong—a moment that should have turned toward redemption, but instead collapses in on itself. The Ring gets picked up, not thrown away. And no Gollum-figure stumbles into the fire this time. Just a man, an arsenal of weapons, and multiple hospital floors full of corpses.

## SOMETHING TO FIGHT FOR
### Joel as the Man with No Choice

At the end of the blood-soaked day, we don't walk out of that hospital with Marlene. We don't commiserate with the "heroic" Fireflies or linger over a surgical table with quiet moral anguish. We walk out with Joel amidst the mess and mayhem we helped him create. And if we're being honest, most of us do it without hesitation. Because while the Fireflies make a choice for Ellie, despite everything, Joel still feels like her protector. He's her "dad," no matter how much he has tried to fight against that role throughout most of their journey. And for a man who has already lost one daughter, the idea of losing yet another is simply unthinkable. His act that day isn't about saving the world. Deep down, this is about Sarah as much as anything else.

Because two decades earlier, Joel begged a soldier to spare his baby girl's life. And the fucking asshole didn't. And now, here he is again. Only this time, Joel has the gun. This time, Joel is the one giving the orders. And this time, not a single motherfucker in this godforsaken world is going to take her from him. Not again.

So, he slaughters every... last... one of them.

Not because he's evil. Not because he's noble. But because he's broken. Because he's tired. Because he knows too well what the abyss of grief looks like and he's unwilling to spend another second there. Not that he couldn't survive there—no!—because *he knows he could*. He just doesn't want to (and who could blame him?).

The weight of such a reality matters. This isn't some Boris and Natasha supervillain who twirls his mustache and chooses ruin for fun. This is a man so haunted by loss, so hollowed out by decades of failure, that saving Ellie isn't a moral calculus; it's muscle memory from a time long ago. As a father, it's still his instinct. It's what he does because it's the only thing left in him *to do*—fight for the light, and Joel's light *is* Ellie. And while some of us may cringe at the piles of bodies left in his wake, we understand the whole mess. We "get it." We recognize that this is how grief works, and that most of us would do the very same thing if it came down to our "baby girl."

So, where does that leave us?

On one side we have the Fireflies, the self-anointed saviors high on the opium of utilitarian morality. On the other we have Joel, a grieving father on a warpath, trying to outrun the ghost of a teenage girl from Austin. Both sides convinced they're doing what's right. Both sides play god. And both sides are willing to erase Ellie in the process.

That's what makes this moment in Salt Lake City so devastating. Because neither party gets to be the hero. Here, the Fireflies are Boromir, grasping at power—not to hoard it, but to wield it "in the hour of need." To turn the Ring toward some great and noble end. But Tolkien warned us about what happens when even the well-meaning place it on their finger: it bends them, stretched thinner than butter scraped over too much bread,[6] contorted toward a posture no different than that of its maker, Sauron. "Let the Ring be your weapon," Boromir says. And that's what the Fireflies do. They desire to break Ellie down into her most basic parts—literally—to wield her like a weapon against *Cordyceps*, sacrificing her without consent for a salvation no one can guarantee.

And Joel? Joel does the same. Not with a sanitized scalpel or clinical microscope, but with gunpowder, rage, and unresolved trauma. Not to save *the* world, but, as I've said multiple times already, to save *his* world. And that is precisely the tragedy: that even love, when laced with trauma, can become a form of control. That even loyalty and devotion can metastasize into violence.

Neither the Fireflies nor Joel are Frodo. Frodo, who carries the burden of the Ring to the precipice of the Cracks without yielding to it. Frodo, who can see past the illusion of power (if only barely). In *The Last of Us*, we are given no such hero. We are given no Frodo Baggins. No Samwise the Brave. No noble and upstanding Hobbits. And no Gandalf returning from some ethereal place beyond the confines of Arda. Just broken people, doing the best they can with the wreckage they've been handed.

Joel's story is not the triumph of the grizzled hero. It is the funeral of such a concept. The symbolic death of the "good guy" trope. The idea that someone, somewhere, will make all the "right" choices when it matters most. A traditional story can be spun by such an image, but that myth is buried beneath the hospital floor right next to the lie Joel tells Ellie after she wakes up. Because when all is said and done, the most "heroic" thing anyone could have done at that point is tell the truth. And no one—not the doctors, not the scientists, not even the father-figure whom Ellie loves—makes such a choice.

## SOMEONE TO FIGHT AGAINST
### Abby and Ellie as Reflections in Blood

In a different timeline, Abby and Ellie would have been allies. Perhaps friendly rivals or maybe even true friends. They're both clever, resilient, and fiercely loyal to the people they love (some might say to a fault). And correct me if I'm wrong, but they both even love dogs! However, in *their* world, the one ravaged by *Cordyceps* and perennial pursuits of power, they are not companions. Rather, these two women are orbiting shadows, drawn into each other's gravity by the deaths of the same men. And because of that, they become both bitter enemies and mimetic doubles.

*Part II* dares to challenge us with an uncomfortable truth of the universe: that enemies aren't often opposites; they are twins. In fact, Abby and Ellie's stories are so tightly wound together that they might as well be chapters of the same book. They both lose father figures. They both go on quests for revenge. They both kill and maim people they never thought they would (or could) harm. And in the end, both are left in ruin—scarred, haunted, traumatized, and utterly alone.

Abby's story in *Part II* begins where Ellie's ends, with the chance for revenge. When she hunts down and brutally murders Joel outside Jackson, she does exactly what we assume Ellie will later do to her. Abby finishes the job. She takes Joel out. She stares down the man who killed her father and makes him pay for it. Slowly. Brutally. Horrifically. We hate her for it... at first. But that's the genius of the game. It makes us hate her, then it forces us to play *as* her. It makes us feel her pain, her guilt, her longing for something akin to redemption. And my God does it succeed! Because by the end of the game, we don't want Ellie to kill Abby. We want her to go home to Dina (if that's even on the table at that point).

Thankfully, Ellie *does* stop. Unlike Abby, who finishes the job when the moment arrives, Ellie lets the moment pass. On a blood-soaked beach in Santa Barbara, Ellie finally sees what the rest of us began to suspect long ago: that vengeance never brings closure. That killing Abby will never bring Joel back. That violence only begets more violence until it swallows the world whole.[7] And so, Ellie walks away. Like Frodo, she loses a finger—two, actually. She loses her family. She nearly loses her very humanity. But she finally walks away.

Does that make Ellie the "better" person? And Abby the villain? If you've read this far, you know that's not how any of this works.

The moral architecture of *The Last of Us* is not concerned with the stark binaries of philosophical fundamentalism. Good vs. evil? Hero vs. villain? Such systematic scaffolding collapsed back in 2013. Instead, what we see in Ellie and Abby is a portrait of mimetic rivalry, one drawn straight from the pages of Girard. As the French anthropologist observed, "Competitors are fundamentally those who run or walk together, rivals those who dwell on opposite banks of the same river."[8] And this is what Abby and Ellie are: mirrors, as reflections in a pool of water. They aren't at odds with one another because they are different; they fight like hell because they are too alike. They are each caught in an infinite feedback loop of pain, vengeance, and the desire to make "the other" suffer in the way "I" have suffered. This is the very heart of mimetic theory.

Again, in a different life, Ellie and Abby might have high-fived over a successful clicker headshot, argued about the best guitar riffs, traded stories over lost loved ones, and maybe even teamed up to take down FEDRA.[9] But in this universe, there's simply too much pain, too much history, and too much mirrored rage.

Thankfully, however, despite all of that, both choose not to perpetuate that rage. At the desperate behest of Lev, Abby spares Dina in the basement of a theatre in Seattle. Later, Ellie returns the favor and stops just short of drowning Abby on a beach in California. And in doing so, they both sever the never-ending cycle of violence that grips all of us. Not because Ellie and Abby are saints, not because they have found some neat theological answer to their pain, but because something in them breaks—or maybe heals—just enough for them to choose something else. Something freer. Something *human*.

And that, like telling the truth in the face of loss, might just be the only other thing loosely resembling heroism in the post-apocalyptic hellhole these two women live in. It's not victory, but simply the refusal to continue the cycle of violence that has gripped humanity since its inception.

## WHAT'S LEFT OF THE LIGHT
## Toward a New Kind of Heroism

> "Sometimes the biggest heroes don't wear capes or armor, nor do they wield a broadsword; instead, they wear green and yellow tunics, walk around on bare feet, and can still surprise us decades after thinking we've learned all their ways."[10]
>
> — **MATTHEW J. DISTEFANO**, *The Wisdom of Hobbits*

So, if there are no saints, and all the sinners are merely survivors who have happened to endure up to this point, where does that leave us? If Joel's brutal paternal instinct and the Fireflies' utilitarian idealism both fail the test of heroism—even when we can all resonate with both—and if Ellie and Abby cancel each other out in the mirrored madness of mimetic revenge, are we left with nothing but the ashes of pure nihilism?

Not quite.

Because the brilliance of this story is not that it kills off the heroic good guy, it's that it dares to challenge the need for a hero in the first place. And if there *is* something like a hero—though I challenge the need to use such a word—it isn't someone who storms a hospital or throws the first punch. It's the one who lays down the weapon and walks away. Not from responsibility, but from the insatiable hunger for control. The one who refuses to perpetuate the same cycles of violence that destroyed them in the first place.

Undoubtedly, I don't mean to sanctify anyone in this story. Joel is still a liar. Abby is still a murderer. Ellie still abandons her family in the pursuit of "justice" (read: vengeance). All the characters we have looked at are deeply flawed. But they are also capable of doing things some of us have an impossible time doing, which is seeing their own reflection in the enemy. And when they see themselves, they hesitate, which allows just enough light to filter through the cracks of their soul. It may not be the type of blaze my best friend Michael and I have enjoyed during our years of Bonfire Sessions, but it is a faint ember glowing calmly and quietly amidst the drenching Seattle rain.

In *The Wisdom of Hobbits*, I argue that heroism is rooted not in conquest or moral certainty, but in care—care for those around us, for the planet, for *the good* as such. In daring to soften the edges of the modern masculine man, I attempt to put forth a vision of humanity where our greatest strength is not in slaying dragons, but in tending gardens. That to be mighty is not to destroy enemies, but to bear each other's burdens. *The Last of Us* shows us the other side of the same coin of truth: that even in a world where everything is broken, the simple refusal to do more harm can be its own act of heroic grace. That turning back from the edge of the cliff is something far braver than charging into a company of Orcs.

"No half measures," they say. But maybe, in the tragic world of *The Last of Us*, half measures are all we have. Sometimes though, that's enough. The trembling hand that loosens its grip. The jaw unclenched mid-scream. The choice to let someone live when every cell in your body cries out for revenge. Maybe this is what remains of the "good guy" in the ruins of the Old World. They are not someone who swoops in to save the day. They are simply someone who chooses not to harm it further. They do not wear shining armor, but they do choose to love, even if that love comes too late, costs too much, or simply means walking away from hate.

6

# BEYOND THE HORIZON

*The Moral Cost of Community*

*"I don't know what you heard, but you should see the town. We're over twenty families strong now. It was Maria and her father, they set up this place that had the idea of being self-sustained. We got crops and livestock... Remember how we thought that no one could live like this anymore? Well, we're doing it."*[1]

— **TOMMY MILLER**

"Complicated" can be the word that best describes all the themes we've explored to this point. Community—the topic of this chapter—is no different. Community can be like salvation but also a prison. It can keep us alive despite the odds but can damn all of us faster than a horde of perturbed clickers in a narrow hallway. It can harden us toward love and self-sacrifice or calcify us into tribalistic shells of our former selves. Community is both the best of us and the worst of us.

In the world before Outbreak Day, humanity believed that without others we would perish, not just biologically, but psychologically and even spiritually. "It is not good for man to be alone," says the writer of Genesis,[2] and in a very real sense, that's still true in our post-pandemic wasteland. But *The Last of Us* isn't interested in idealistic platitudes, even if they *are* derived from so-called holy writ. This series wants to test the limits of the human imagination by seeing what happens when "not being alone" comes at a profoundly high moral cost. Because make no mistake about it, the communities in this story—from the Rattlers to the Fireflies, from the WLF to the Seraphites, from David's cultic cannibals to the faded-out remnants of the QZs—each is built atop the scaffoldings of power, on something quite ugly, something quite violent, something that, in a previous era, we pretended to be unthinkable. (But who are we kidding? Pre-pandemic societies are just as ugly![3])

Take David, for instance. His little commune of traumatized survivors isn't held together by love or shared values, but rather, by fear, coercion, predation, and—unbeknownst to some of its members—even cannibalism. David doesn't offer hope; he offers meat to starving people. And he justifies it all by wrapping his depravity in a thin spiritual veneer, one that quickly collapses the moment Ellie sees him for who—or rather, *what*—he is: a predator who wraps his violence in a demented and perverted view of the divine will.

By contrast, in a world turned to rot, communities can also become sanctuaries. Tommy and Maria's town offers something stable. Children here laugh and have snowball fights. Food is grown and homecooked meals are prepared. There are armed patrols, of course, but electricity also hums, powering movie nights and holiday dances in the community center. These seemingly small things matter. Deeply. But again, no community is heaven on earth. Jackson also has rules, expectations, bigots named Seth,[4] and a giant wall that resembles those old medieval towns from centuries long ago.

So, what's our initial takeaway? Is community a blessing or a curse? A necessity or a liability? A moral good or a pragmatic survival strategy?

The answer, of course, is... *yes.*

Remember, this is *The Last of Us*, so everything is complex. And maybe that's the whole point. Maybe the greatest tension in this beautiful and gut-wrenching series isn't whether individuals can survive, but whether they can survive together without losing the fragile thread of their humanity in the process. Because, as we'll see in the sections that follow, the question we should be asking ourselves isn't merely how people build and sustain communities in a post-apocalyptic hellscape; but how they can live with the things those communities make them do.

## THE FRAGILE MYTH OF TOGETHERNESS

As much as we in the United States love to romanticize the rugged individualism of survivalists like Bill—with his canned beans, trip wires, homemade nail bombs, and precisely zero friends—the truth of the matter is far less cinematic: we *need* people. We need community. We are, as the mimetic theorists have rightly posited, deeply interdependent creatures.[5] We are formed by those around us and those we take on as models. Without others, we don't become independent but we do run the risk of becoming fucking monsters.

And yet, when we do band together, we bring all our baggage with us. Our prejudices. Our inadequacies. Our bigotries. Our desire for power. Our need for violence. Our ideologies, borders, rules, leaders, scapegoats, rituals, dogma, warfare, and yes, even our figurative and literal cannibalism.

Across two games, we are introduced to a range of factions and communities attempting, in their own uniquely horrifying ways, to create some version of "civilization." Some try to recreate the Old World, some reject it entirely, and others try to rise above it all through brute force, fundamentalist religion, or a morally-justified and well-timed revolution. All of them fail in their own way, but each, in its collapse or corruption, reveals something about who we all are, what we're willing to compromise, who we're willing to sacrifice, and what we're willing to believe so that we can endure and survive together.

Let's take a tour, shall we?

## FEDRA and the QZs: Authoritarianism with a Dash of Bureaucracy

Twenty years after the outbreak, the Federal Disaster Response Agency, or FEDRA, is essentially all that is left of the United States government.[6] After the *Cordyceps* pandemic obliterates civil society, FEDRA steps in to build Quarantine Zones (QZs) and enforce order through martial law. Think FEMA, if FEMA was also the TSA, the CIA, the DOJ, ICE, and a dystopian wet dream of Dick Cheney, or, worse yet, Stephen Miller and Donald J. Trump.

From the outside looking in, FEDRA zones look like the last bastions of civilization. Children attend school. Grownups work jobs. But that's about the extent of the good. Peel back the layers and all you'll find is corruption: executions without any semblance of due process and an overtly fascistic rule of law. FEDRA claim to provide safety, but it's a type of safety purchased through subjugation. In FEDRA's world, community means control, it means blindly trusting authority—*their authority*. Obey the chain of command. Do your job. Shut the fuck up and don't ask questions. Snitch on your neighbor if there's even a hint of rebellion.

What FEDRA shows us, first and foremost, is the dark side of centralized power. When community is built solely around compliance, fear becomes the glue that holds it all together. But fear, as it turns out, is a terrible long-term solution, as you can only fill so many cracks, patch so many holes, or mend so many worn out pages of your society before the whole thing crumbles in front of you.

## The Fireflies: Revolution and a Scalpel

Standing in direct opposition to FEDRA is the resistance group known as the Fireflies. This ragtag resistance fighter operation are equal parts revolutionaries, idealists, and black-hooded insurgents who believe in rebuilding the world through, among other things, bioethics violations.

The Fireflies are nothing if not a fascinating case of moral absolutism. They claim to desire freedom, but it's a case of *freedom for me but not for thee*. It's their narrative and they want control of the whole damn thing. It's their version of the cure. Like a certain red-hat-wearing autocrat, *they are the only ones who can do it*. Their doctor is the only human on the planet smart enough to pull it off (I guess all other physicians are either dead or infected?). So, when Ellie falls into their lap, they don't hesitate to trade her life for humanity's redemption. *Fuck consent, am I right, Dr. Anderson?*

Their motto is literally, "look for the light," but in practice, the Fireflies have joined the dark side a long time ago. If FEDRA is the empire, the Fireflies are the rebellion. The only problem is that they stop being subversive the moment they gain access to power. Which tells us something hauntingly familiar: the revolution, too, can become the oppressor.[7]

## The Washington Liberation Front: The Military Industrial Complex, but Make It Relatable

Right on time, we have the WLF (or "Wolves," for those who love a good moniker). Originally a liberation movement revolting against FEDRA's rule in Seattle, the WLF ousts their oppressors before promptly building a new system that looks an awful lot like the one they just overthrew.

*Meet the new boss, same as the old boss.*

The WLF's guiding principle is strength through power. They put boots on the ground and guns in the hands of men and women who know how to pull a trigger. Their leadership is militaristic, hierarchal, and centralized. They view the world in the most brutally pragmatic ways. Dogs aren't pets; they sniff out the enemy. Teenage years aren't for fooling around with a summer fling or experimenting with a little weed; they are for preparing the mind and body for the machine of war.

And yet, the members of the WLF do experience a degree of normalcy. Some soldiers can be overheard talking about *Harry Potter*, while Abby is seen reading David Benioff's *City of Thieves*.[8] Food is grown and children attend school in the somewhat friendly confines of Soundview Stadium. The people who live here joke, flirt, and fall in and out of love—all the normal stuff people do. They aren't monsters. They're just people who believe that safety and violence must go hand in hand. And that, too, is a lesson in human nature.

Like many real-world militarized communities, the WLF justifies its methods by the world it believes it inhabits, a world where anything less than total power means certain death. Ironically, it's in this pursuit of power that most of them die on that fateful night on the Seraphite island,[9] but isn't that, too, a tale as old as time?

### The Seraphites: Feel Her Love... Or Else

Speaking of the Seraphites (also known as "Scars" according to the "Wolves"). This religious sect emerges in the wake of civilization's collapse and worships a deceased prophet who preached humility, simplicity, and a complete rejection of the pre-pandemic world. No technology. No "modern" conveniences. Just classic doomsday cultish vibes and what seems like an entire language based on whistling. To the Seraphites, technology is corruption, cities are sin, and the mechanized gears of industry are blasphemy. So, these "disciples" live in harmony with nature, don humble robes, and communicate via ominous whistles that echo through the trees like haunted wind chimes.

But let's not mistake this pastoralism for peace. These folks are far removed from Tolkien's Hobbits and the idyllic Shire. The Seraphites enforce their rigid religious rites through executions, public hangings, and the brutal mutilation of anyone who deviates from their creeds. Women are especially subjugated and those who challenge their binary gender codes are hunted down as heretics and apostates.

Their community is one built on purity and enforced by terror. And their religion, while rooted in some truly beautiful ideals, has long since metastasized into authoritarian dogma just like so many faith traditions that have come before it.[10]

## David's Group: Religion, Cannibalism, and Predation

Did someone say, "authoritarian dogma?" Great, because David's community is the result of combining the fundamentalism of a Southern Baptist Sunday School with Hannibal Lecter. At first glance, David presents as a calm and rational man. A born leader. To his flock, he is their shepherd. But when he first meets Ellie, his flock is starving, and his sermons aren't exactly FDA-approved.

After losing their food supply to the harshness of winter, David's group resorts to cannibalism. Worse still, David himself is a sexual predator who attempts to groom and dominate Ellie (who is fourteen at the time). His community is built not on consent or respect for women and girls, or even shared beliefs and morals; it's built on fear, hunger, and quiet compliance in the face of great evil.

David reminds us that not all communities are built for mutual aid. Some are simply cults. Full stop. And if you're ever unsure whether your local post-apocalyptic commune is leaning toward the dark side, just ask: *Are we eating people yet?* That should be a tell-tale sign that something has gone completely sideways and perhaps it's time to find a new leader, one who isn't trying to push themselves onto girls who are years below the age of consent.

But that's the nature of predation, isn't it? If people are hungry, they will look the other way when confronted by its evil. They will look past the red flags, past the moments that make them cringe. They will witness who their cult leader is, but they won't *see* because they don't want to. And in their quiet acquiescence they condone the worst of the worst all in the name of the survival of the community.

## The Hunters and the Rattlers: Survival Without Illusion

The final two antagonistic groups we will mention are the Hunters and the Rattlers—factions who make no pretense about what they are. The Hunters of Pittsburgh and the Rattlers of Santa Barbara aren't trying to rebuild society; they are *all* about survival.

That's it.

Each group kills outsiders indiscriminately. Both take what they want. And neither thinks twice about turning people into slaves, bait, and even meat for clickers. Their moral codes are simple, if we can even call them that: protect your own and fuck everyone else. No dogma and no manifestos. Just guns, grit, and grievous conduct that strips all involved of their shared humanity.

These are the communities that emerge when all pretense is stripped away, when survival becomes the only value left. When we stumble upon them, we are horrified not because they are alien, but because they are *all of us* when there is nothing left to lose and no one left to love.

## Jackson: Utopia (Just Don't Get Too Comfortable)

Of all the communities in *The Last of Us*, Jackson—run by Tommy and Maria—is the one that actually works. The town has power, plumbing, patrols, livestock, gardens, and a school. The community center hosts movie nights, children have snowball fights, and the citizens even celebrate Christmas.

But don't let the Norman Rockwell exterior fool you. Jackson isn't heaven. It's a heavily guarded fortress that only works because it has walls, rules, codes of conduct, and a hell of a lot of bullets. Exile is always a possibility for those who step too far out of line. Kids don't get to just play with snowballs; they have to be handy with rifles and handguns, too. And LGBTQ folks who never even knew the Old World still have to deal with baked-in bigotry and homophobia.[11]

Jackson is what you get when a community attempts to rebuild with intentionality, and yet, still must play by the rules of a world gone mad. Of course, teenage kids must be ready to arm themselves at a moment's notice! There are hordes of infected and violent mobs of survivors beyond the town's walls. Their lives—and indeed the lives of every one of its members—are as close to idealism as the universe allows, but even here, morality is conditional and survival still hangs in the balance.

So, what does all this tell us? We've just surveyed every flavor of post-apocalyptic community this story has to offer—militant, religious, revolutionary, familial—and if you're feeling morally exhausted, good. That's kind of the point. Because, for all their differences, each faction isn't just a survival mechanism, they're a mirror. And what they reflect is far more unsettling than even the gnarliest bloater. They reflect *us*.

## ONE CATASTROPHE AWAY
### The Fragile Order of Tribalism

> "People are tempted to multiply [...] innocent victims, to kill all the enemies of the nation or the class [...] and to sing the praises of murder and madness."[12]
>
> — **RENÉ GIRARD**,
> *Things Hidden Since the Foundation of the World*

Every community in *The Last of Us*—from the militant, to the mythic, to the quietly agrarian—tells us something uncomfortably honest about ourselves. Strip away the infected and what we're left with is a mirror held up to human civilization as it *currently* stands: fragile, territorial, and just one bad Thursday away from utter collapse.

Because let's not kid ourselves, humans are tribal creatures. We have always drawn boundaries between "us" and "them," whether by bloodline, belief, or baseball team (go Red Sox!). It's how we establish some sort of identity, how we create meaning, and, if we're being perfectly honest, how we give ourselves permission to treat outsiders like problems to be solved or pests to be eradicated. Every faction in this world reveals this tendency. They are just wrapped in different costumes. The Fireflies have their martyr complex. The WLF have their Boromir-with-the-Ring spirit. The Seraphites have their puritanical codes and rites. And the Hunters? They've got meat to eat and zero fucks to give. No matter the paint job, the engine is the same: *protect your own at any cost*.

In all fairness, some of this behavior is necessary. When everything collapses, people do what they can to rebuild order from the ruins. But order always comes at a cost, and the more rigid the structure, the more likely it is to splinter under pressure.[13] FEDRA's military zones collapse because authoritarianism without empathy breeds insurrection. The Fireflies implode because idealism left unchecked becomes just another excuse for a savior complex. The WLF becomes indistinguishable from the tyranny it once resisted in FEDRA. The Seraphites devour themselves under the weight of their own piety and hypocrisy. And David's camp... well, that's simply what you get when the illusion of civilization is managed by a predator in sheep's clothing.

What is the lesson here? That no matter how noble the creed, how moving the anthem, or how morally upright the mission statement is on paper, every human system is built atop a ticking timebomb. We are all one catastrophe away from becoming zealots, from turning cannibal, and from telling ourselves it's okay to kill a kid if it might save our own. So, it's not that these factions are monstrous by nature. It's that every human community, even the most well-intentioned, carries the seed of collapse within it. All it takes is fear, hunger, or grief to crack the façade of order and unleash the old mimetic impulse to find an enemy to blame, a scapegoat to sacrifice, or a child to put under the knife for "the greater good."

That's the bleak truth this world reveals, but thankfully, there's more to the story. Not everything is entirely pessimistic and there is indeed some *hope* in all this.

## AND YET...
## The Tie that Binds

We've seen the blood on the walls. We've witnessed what happens when tribes harden into armies, when values calcify into dogma, and when the desperate cling to power and call it salvation. We've seen communities that eat their enemies—literally—and others that sacrifice children in the name of a brighter tomorrow. And if we're paying attention, we've also seen how terrifyingly easy it is for any of us to fall into some of those same patterns. But one catastrophe, one betrayal, one whispered lie is all it takes for everything to fall apart.

And yet...

Humans are communal creatures. We always have been. Strip away the fortified stadium bases, religious relics, and hastily-constructed perimeter fences, and what you'll find beneath it all is the aching need to belong to something bigger than ourselves. We are born with a need not just to survive, but to survive and thrive *together*. Because even in a world teetering on the brink—hell, maybe *especially* in a world teetering on the brink—it is community that keeps the thread from snapping. It's the story we tell ourselves about who we are and who we want to be. And that story only works when it's shared.

We see this in the community of Jackson. Yes, it's imperfect. Yes, there are boundaries and guns and bigotry and secrets, but are also moments of laughter, intimate dancing, couples falling in love, Taylor guitars being strummed, and pothead electricians wiring hidden rooms for grow lights. In Jackson, there are tomatoes. And my God, can you imagine the taste of a post-apocalyptic, fresh-grown Brandywine tomato?

As I've said before, Jackson is not a utopia, but it's something worth protecting. Rather than being built on control, it's built on shared contribution. It's what civilization can be when we resist the slide into tribalism and instead choose interdependence over ideology and community over capitalism. In short, Jackson is a town of people really trying to live not just *with* one another, but *for* one another.

Still, let's not get too comfortable.

Because if Joel's story reminds us of anything, it's that comfort breeds complacency. And in a world such as this, that's all it takes for the next collapse to begin. *The Last of Us* never lets us forget that all these structures we build are just that—*structures*. Constructs. Make believe systems of subjectivity. The wind howls, the earth shakes, and the whole goddamn thing comes crashing down. That's what makes community so beautiful and terrible at the same time: its fragility.

But fragility doesn't mean futility. In the ruins, there's still music to be played. There's still the laughter of children. There are still people who, like Ellie and Dina, dance in barns and hook up in old grow houses. Still those who open their gates, share their bread, bury their dead, and plant their vegetable seeds. Still those who resist the dehumanizing pull of vengeance and mimetic tribal rage to instead build something so profanely divine as a greenhouse in the snow.

In one of the game's rare moments of tenderness, Ellie whispers, "After all we've been through. Everything I've done. It can't be for nothing."[14] That is the refrain of the post-apocalyptic community. It's not about perfection; it's about perseverance. It's about fighting tooth and nail for something resembling love, praying all the while that we don't strip away anyone's humanity in the process.

# 7

# You Can't Stop This

*Revenge, Justice, and an Endless Cycle*

"*You stupid old man... You don't get to rush this.*"[1]

— **ABBY ANDERSON**

Vengeance is not just something we feel. It is a force that shapes the world, a disease to go alongside the *Cordyceps* fungus. Which is more powerful? It's difficult to tell. Both spread. Both imitate. Both infect even those with the noblest intentions, rotting them to the core. Vengeance surreptitiously dresses everything it does up as justice, and in doing so, just like the infected who lose their minds to the fungus, our favorite characters lose their hearts and souls to the lie that revenge can ever set things to right.

Because of Joel's slaughter of the Fireflies in Salt Lake City, the entire story in *Part II* becomes a meditation on what happens when we mistake vengeance for justice, and justice for healing. But here's the rub: we are never asked to judge the characters for their violence, only to understand them. Worse yet, the game dares us to relate to it by seeing ourselves in it. And if we're honest, we do.

If you've read my 2017 book *From the Blood of Abel* or otherwise understand the root causes of mimetic violence, you already know where I'm going. Shortly after one of the writers of the biblical book of Genesis details the second creation narrative,[2] we are confronted with mimetic violence and vengeance. The Lamechian brutishness of Genesis 4 that leads to Noah's flood is initiated when Cain kills Abel, not because Abel wronged him in any way, but because Abel became a rival. Remember, mimetic rivalry isn't born from difference; rather, it is birthed out of two key elements: *sameness* and *proximity*.[3] It spawns from the unbearable feeling that someone close to you has something you cannot attain. So you kill. You scapegoat. You eliminate the one who reminds you of what you lack. And then, to stop the cycle from coming full circle, you prohibit the thing itself and mythologize the originary event,[4] spinning an account that makes your violence seem justified, necessary, and divine even.[5]

*The Last of Us*, however, doesn't let us mythologize any events in this manner. Instead, it strips the cycle of vengeance bare and exposes it as what it is: *a lie*.

We watch as Abby kills Joel with a golf club. It's an image so jarringly visceral that it has etched itself into our retinas like *Cordyceps* spores on the brain. Then, the game does something quite enigmatic, forcing us to live *with* Abby. To play *as* Abby. To *know* Abby's pain. But just when we begin to understand her loss, we're thrust back into Ellie's rage. Controller in hand, we feel Ellie's thirst for revenge, and slowly, methodically, begin to understand that both women are victims of the same gravitational pull initiated by two brothers long ago.[6] They are each Cain and Abel. Each Romulus and Remus. Each the scapegoater and the scapegoated. Each caught in a story far more ancient than them, and far more violent than they deserve.

This chapter is about *that* story. It is about how violence perpetuates itself through imitation, how justice mutates into retribution, and finally, how mercy can interrupt all of it. We'll begin with Joel, the hinge on which this particular point of the vengeance cycle swings. He is both the savior and the sinner, the father and the executioner. In saving Ellie, he potentially damns everyone else, making himself the target of a retribution he cannot escape. We'll then explore Ellie's descent. Not as a villain, but as a wounded daughter grasping at a world that no longer makes sense. Her path is paved with dead bodies, but also with broken prayers to a God she doesn't believe in, half-written songs on polished Taylor guitars, and haunted by ghosts she cannot put to rest. Finally, we'll walk with Abby to understand what it means to achieve the goal of revenge and still not be made whole. Because that's the paradox of vengeance, isn't it? Even when you win, you lose. Even when your enemies are dead, your grief remains.

## RIPPLES IN BLOOD
## The Unfolding Waves of Vengeance

### The First Wave: Joel, the Mimetic Trigger

It's tempting to view Joel's final act in Salt Lake City as the genesis of the cycle of vengeance in *The Last of Us*. After all, it's the catalytic moment that leads to Abby's warpath and Ellie's unraveling in *Part II*. But let's be honest with ourselves: Joel didn't start this fire. He just added fuel to a flame that's been burning since the dawn of humanity.

Joel, like all of us, is the product of circumstances. He is a man shaped by a collapsing world, a father who watches his teenage daughter bleed out in his arms after a soldier, acting under despotic orders, fires a round into her stomach. That moment doesn't just destroy Joel's sense of order; it burns down any notion of justice he might have been carrying. What replaces it is pure, unfiltered survivalism where the ends always justify the means.

The lie vengeance tells us is that it will restore order by fixing what's broken and giving us back what we've lost. But all vengeance does is give birth to more vengeance. "I have killed [...] a young man for striking me," says Lamech in Genesis 4. The result is a humanity filled with so much violence that the text goes on to tell us, "all flesh has corrupted its ways upon the earth."[7]

Which God then mimetically responds to with even more violence: "I have determined to make an end of all flesh, for the earth is filled with violence because of them; now I am going to destroy them along with the earth."[8] In other words, "because humanity's violence is so corrupt, so wicked, so evil," says the Lord, "I am going to mimetically engage in the war to end all wars and flood the whole damn thing."

Likewise, Joel is mimetic through and through. To suggest that his actions in the final chapter of *Part I* exist in a vacuum would be incorrect. And it would be far too reductive to chalk it all up to him merely becoming evil. Joel does what he does because he is a mirror, a reflection, an echo of every trauma that has come before. Of Sarah, of the years in the Boston QZ, of every nameless body he and Tommy left behind during their years as Hunters. Joel kills not just to protect Ellie, but to attempt to redeem his own failure with Sarah. In doing this, he becomes the unwitting architect of everything that follows in *Part II*. Undoubtedly, Abby doesn't become a killer in a vacuum either. Because of Joel's actions, she becomes what Joel had become: grief incarnate. This is the gut-punch of the entire cycle. Vengeance is never comprised of just one isolated act. It doesn't stop with a dead doctor or beloved protagonist, just like it didn't stop with Lamech's nameless victim. Someone that day found out their kid had been killed, and if Lamech's vengeance was seventy-sevenfold, then my guess is that parent's rage was a million times more. Violence echoes, as all good myths show, and it's not a difficult task to follow the line of dead bodies all the way back to the beginning.

## The Second Wave: Ellie and the Cost of Retaliation

When Ellie is held down by the Salt Lake Crew and forced to watch Joel's murder at the hands of Abby, something in her breaks. Something she can't quite name and can never quite fix. In her breaking, Ellie makes a vow to hunt down *every single motherfucker* involved and make them suffer: "I'm gonna find... and I'm gonna kill... every last one of them."[9] This, she believes, will set things to right.

But vengeance doesn't ever accomplish anything productive, and in fact only makes things worse. Deep down, Ellie must know this. And yet, she still straps on her pack, sharpens her knife, and walks out of her peaceful-adjacent life, not once, but twice—the second time, leaving Dina, JJ, and any possibility of healing behind. Because vengeance, like a virus, replicates itself inside its host, convincing them that closure is just one dead body away.

Only it never is.

Ellies great tragedy, then, is not that she fails to get revenge on Abby, but that she nearly succeeds. She becomes everything she hates, and then some. Bodies are left in her wake—Nora, Owen, a pregnant Mel, all the names of those WLF soldiers we can no longer remember.[10] And in heading down this path, Ellie loses herself, bit by bit, piece by piece, until the only thing left is a hollow shell of the girl who once danced in a Wyoming barn and told dorky jokes from a pun book.

She tells herself she is doing this for Joel, but we all know he would never have wanted this for her. Not another "baby girl" being lost to the continuous cycle of corrosive human violence. Because Joel, for all his flaws, still held onto love. He still regularly strummed his guitar and imagined himself becoming a famous singer. He still made time for coffee and art and dumb-ass jokes. But after he is gone, Ellie barely does any of this. That's what makes the scene in Seattle's Valiant Music Shop so touching, and why to this day I can't hear her version of "Take on Me" without welling up with tears. So often, Ellie is burning through Seattle like a forest fire and torching whatever fragile intimacy she had begun to build with Dina in the process.

And still, it's not enough.

Because again, vengeance is never enough. Mimetic theory shows us this. The endless parade of rivals we hate are often the people we most resemble. Cain doesn't kill some stranger from a foreign land; he kills his brother. Ellie doesn't desire to kill Abby because she is so different; she wants to kill her because they are the same. Two broken daughters in a broken world, chasing ghosts, killing memories, each a reflection of the other's rage.

That's what makes the scene at the beach in Santa Barbara so haunting. It should be the final act, the final reckoning, the moment Ellie "wins." But instead, we're given a scene so grotesque and sad it barely feels like vengeance at all. More like killing yourself slowly while staring into a mirror.

And yet, Ellie stops short. Though wounded, missing two fingers, and unable to grip her knife, Ellie still has the chance to finish Abby beneath the shallow waves of the Pacific. But she doesn't follow through, and in doing so, breaks the cycle she has been a part of for so long. She permits Abby to take Lev to Catalina before picking herself up and trekking back to Wyoming to figure out what, if anything, is left of her former life.

## The Third Wave: Abby and the Aftermath of Victory

Ellie stops short. Abby doesn't. She rides the wave of vengeance all the way to shore, killing our most beloved protagonist. And yet, despite "winning," she ends up just as lost, just as wrecked, and more alone than when she began.

To be clear, Abby's quest isn't inherently more or less righteous than Ellie's. Chronologically her violence precedes Ellie's, but mimetically it ironically mirrors Joel's. She is, of course, not some deranged villain hellbent on cruelty. She is a daughter mourning her father, a soldier molded by a war she never asked to be a part of. And when Joel caves in her world by caving in her father's skull, she does what humans have always done: she retaliates. Lamech-style. Seventy-sevenfold. With a nine iron.

And what does Abby get for her troubles? Victory, yes, but at the expense of nearly everything else. All her friends either die or leave her, and the nightmares continue. Because here's the thing: you can kill the bastard who hurt you, but it won't un-kill your grief. It won't reset the clock or bring back what was lost.

What can and does bring you back to wholeness is change toward *the good*. For Abby, this happens slowly at first. A conversation here. A growing sense of disillusionment with WLF's leadership there. A rescue mission she is under no obligation to undertake. But what starts as a ripple turns into a tsunami when Abby, suffering from a crippling fear of heights, descends floor upon floor and into the depths of the hospital to face off against the Rat King—an amalgamation of every festering fear, trauma, and horror the world has to offer. This is the point where everything shifts for her, because all that she does she does it *for* Yara and no one else.

The basement of the hospital is, quite literally, hell. There is no light, no clean way through, and no backup coming. But Abby goes anyway, not because she's forced to or wants to prove her mettle, but because a child needs her. And in those moments, something shifts. She finds the health kit, sure, but more than that, she finds purpose. She finds the thing vengeance can never offer. She finds the chance to save a life rather than ending one. In a very real sense, that is what is meant by *sōzō*—Greek for salvation[11]—not as an escape from death but as the mending of what's broken. To be made whole again.

The irony, no doubt, is that Yara still dies. But even in that, Abby refuses to unravel, because her transformation isn't contingent upon success. Instead, it is rooted in love. Her recurring nightmares don't end because she killed the man who killed her father. They end because she loves someone else more than she hates anyone. Incidentally, that's why she doesn't want to fight Ellie in the end. It's not because she is in a weakened state, physically or mentally, but because she's healed enough to let go.

# BREAKING THE WAVE
## Mercy, Memory, and the Long Walk Home

> "The best revenge is to be unlike him
> who performed the injury."[12]
>
> — **MARCUS AUELIUS**, *Meditations*

Vengeance is a wave, and like any wave, it builds, it crashes, and it has the potential to destroy. But eventually, it recedes.

When we last see Abby, she is on the brink of death, emaciated and broken. The war is over, her vengeance long since complete, and yet, there is no victory parade and no medals. Just a battered skiff, a quiet boy named Lev, and the open sea ahead. The horizon is uncertain, but the blood has been washed away because Abby learned to walk away.

When we last see Ellie—what's left of her anyway—she too has walked away. A few of her fingers are gone, her song is unfinished, and her family has moved on, but she does return home, alone but not empty. Because she chooses mercy. Finally.

And that is the whole damn point. You don't win by getting even. You stop the bleeding by refusing to become the mirror image of what has hurt you.

Throughout *Part II*, Ellie and Abby each stand on the precipice of utter annihilation, fully capable of ending the other. And yet, they don't. Like Frodo and Sam whilst on their trek to Mordor, or Bilbo by the lake in the heart of the Misty Mountains, they are each given the chance to destroy someone "wretched." And like Bilbo, Ellie comes so very close to doing just that. But then she remembers an image of Joel not bleeding out in front of her, but one where he's playing the guitar on his front porch. And in that moment, she lets the Ring fall. Not into the lava, but into the water, the sand, and the silence.

In *The Lord of the Rings*, it is mercy, not might, that saves Middle-earth. Pity, Tolkien calls it. Pity that Bilbo has for Gollum. Pity that Frodo inherits, even if reluctantly. "It was pity that stayed his hand," Gandalf reminds the Hobbit, "Pity, and Mercy: not to strike without need."[13] And here, in the gutted world of *The Last of Us*, we witness echoes of the same truth. Pity is what stays Abby's hand in the theater. Mercy is what stays Ellie's on the beach. They don't become Frodo, nor Gollum either. They come close—closer than any of us would like to admit. But in the end, they drop the weapon, and that is how the wave finally breaks upon the shore. Not with triumph, or traditional closure, or some scripted Hollywood moment of reconciliation, but with a quiet and barely noticed act of mercy. And for a game so drenched in blood, such an ending, however fragile and fleeting, feels a hell of a lot like eucatastrophe.

*8*

# OKAY

*The Weight of Lies and the Price of Truth*

"*Swear to me. Swear to me that everything that you said about the Fireflies is true.*"[1]

**— ELLIE WILLIAMS**

What is truth? Is it a collection of verifiable facts? Is it something that corresponds to objective reality, like a square footage appraisal or accurate headcount of your chickens to make sure none have escaped? Is it in recalling what actually happened on a particular day at a particular time and particular location, as if eyewitnesses aren't constantly wrong and memories aren't the most unreliable narrator of all?

Or is truth something else entirely? Something, dare we say, moral? Because I'll be blunt: if truth is only ever literal, then it is utterly boring. Worse yet, it might even be dangerous.

Imagine, if you will, a German citizen in 1942, asked by SS officers if he is harboring Jews. Now imagine him proudly proclaiming, "Yes! In fact, there's an entire family right beneath the floorboards we stand on!" He would be telling the *literal* truth. And he would be a fucking coward. Not just a coward, but a traitor to human decency. Because in this scenario, telling such a truth gets innocent people killed. Meanwhile, the man who lies and says, "Nope, no Jews here," as his mind's eye darts toward the pantry? He's the one whose moral compass still points north.

So, again I ask: *What is truth?*

And while we're at it: What's a lie? Is a lie simply the withholding of facts? The intentional distortion of reality? If so, is *every* lie immoral? Is it ever wrong to lie to a child? Is it unethical to cushion the unbearable? Or, to flip the question: Is it morally superior to tell the unvarnished truth no matter the consequences?

Of course, the answers to these questions are muddy. Let's not pretend we're sailing the calm waters of the Catalina Channel[2] toward our new home with a regrouped Fireflies. Because lying to your toddler about why the family pet "went to the great farm in the sky" is different than lying about your involvement in unconstitutional human rights violations and child sex trafficking rings. But where, exactly, is the line? Is there a moral "middle ground" ebbing and flowing somewhere between truth and lie?

Quite often, this highly nuanced and morally ambiguous place is where Joel lives. At the end of *Part I*, he makes the decision to save Ellie and thus eliminate the Fireflies, which is something no one can come back from. And to justify that decision, he tells a lie. But what makes Joel's lie significant isn't just the *content* of what he says; it's the *why* behind it. He's not lying to manipulate Ellie for the sake of manipulation. He's lying to save her, or what's left of her, or what Joel convinces *himself* she needs saving from. That's where things get messy.

It's obvious to anyone who has paid close attention that Joel's lie isn't just about the Fireflies or some fantasy cure. It's about Ellie's agency. It's about her right to choose. But also—and I say this not to excuse him, but to understand him—Joel doesn't think she can grasp the weight of what he's done. She's fourteen, and Joel doesn't think she can make a utilitarian decision about sacrificing herself for humanity.

Let's be honest with ourselves and admit that in a sense, he's probably right. Even if Joel tells her the whole truth and nothing but the truth, would Ellie have really understood it? And if she said, "I would've wanted to die," would she have also been okay if Joel then walked out of the hospital and swallowed a bullet after losing yet another daughter? Had such a thought even crossed her mind?

Don't misunderstand me, however. Joel's lie is not what I would consider a moral good. He lies not just to protect Ellie, but to selfishly protect himself. He also believes that love gives him permission to protect her from the truth, and because of this, he suffers the steep cost that comes along with such a decision.

This chapter is about that cost. It's about the fracture that forms when truth is weaponized or withheld. It's about the murky space between facts and meaning, between transparency and care, between brutal honesty and sacred omission. And most of all, it's about the idea that truth is not always redemptive. Sometimes it's nothing more than a jagged shard of reality that cuts deeper the closer you hold it.

So, in what follows, we'll explore the moral ambiguity of Joel's big lie, the fallout that ripples through Ellie's sense of self, and the uncomfortable reality that sometimes no answer is satisfying.

## JOEL'S LIE
## The Weight of the Truth Deferred

In lying to Ellie at the end of *Part I*, Joel builds her a brand-new world, fictionalized of course, laying every single brick himself. "Turns out, there's a whole lot more like you," he deceptively tells her, "People that are immune. There's dozens, actually. Ain't done a damn bit of good neither. They've actually... they've stopped looking for a cure."[3] Though not a real world, this one is quiet, clean, and safe. There are no operating tables or scalpels, and no half-formed apologies either. All told, it is a beautiful lie.

But like all beautiful lies, this one comes with a heavy cost. Because again, this isn't just about whether Joel does a "bad thing." It's about *why* he does it. The man has already watched one daughter die in his arms, has lived through two decades of post-apocalyptic hell, has been betrayed, broken, and bruised under a mountain of ungrieved sorrow and unprocessed trauma, and now, at the end of the journey to Salt Lake City, he's finally found love again. And so, when the choice in the hospital presents itself—*save humanity or save Ellie*—Joel doesn't hesitate. And honestly, who among us would?

But here's where things get complicated. Because Joel's lie isn't just a cover up but a new mythology—their shared story of what normalcy can look like—and once the ink dries there is no going back. There's no chance of "I'll tell her later," because their entire life from that point forward is built upon this very story. In other words, it's built upon *deception*. That's why, when Ellie says, "Swear to me," and Joel responds, "I swear," it lands like a gut punch from a two-time heavyweight champion boxer. We know he's lying. She knows he's lying. We know she knows he's lying. But we also know that she *needs* him to lie. At that moment, she needs the world and her role in it to be simple.

Is Joel *wrong* for creating this fiction? Sure, if that's even the question we want to be answering. But then other questions inevitably spring to mind: Would telling Ellie the truth have been better? Could she have carried the weight of knowing that she was never given a choice? That all adults involved snatched it from her? Could she have forgiven him, or would she have even wanted to?

I don't know, and neither does the game. Hell, neither does Ellie, "though [she] would like to try."[4] All choices are damn-near impossible in *The Last of Us*, and in forcing us to judge its characters we are forced to judge the person staring back at us from a mirror. Because let's be honest and admit that none of us would do any better.

Like so many things in this universe, Joel's lie is a morally paradoxical problem. In one sense, it is a gift. It is a second chance for a girl who never asked to be anyone's savior. But it is also theft, a robbery of agency, a slow-motion betrayal that doesn't detonate until years later after Ellie finally learns the truth. And maybe that's the real question this game wants us to sit with. Is it more moral to tell the truth and destroy someone, or to lie and hold the world together just a little while longer?

Joel chooses the latter, not because he's good, but because he's a flawed human trying to stay connected to the only living being he finds resonance with. One primary problem, though, is that such a connection is secured through faulty means, so it is doomed to crack under the weight of time and its own hypocrisy. And when it does, everything is at risk of completely falling apart.

## ELLIE'S SEARCH FOR TRUTH

There's a moment in *Part II* when the weight of Joel's lie finally crashes down on Ellie. It may seem like it happens suddenly, because in that moment it feels like it, but the quiet ache of memory has long since been rolling toward the shore.

The realization dawns slowly, almost imperceptibly, over the course of the entire second game. But by the time she sits with the memory of their final conversation—the one on the porch where Ellie tells Joel, "I don't think I can ever forgive you... but I'd like to try"[5]—we realize just how deep the rupture has gone. That moment, brief and subdued, is the emotional epicenter of the entire series. Because it's not just about Joel's lie but about everything it steals from Ellie. It's about not having been given the chance to grieve honestly, or the ability to reconcile her disappointment on her own terms.

Joel, in his desperation to protect Ellie from the truth, instead ends up protecting her from closure. Every step Ellie then takes toward vengeance is also a step toward reclaiming her agency, no matter how distorted her view may be. She doesn't just want to make Abby pay for what she does, she wants to understand why Joel did what he did. She wants to understand why she's still angry, still shattered, still half-lost in a life she has never gotten to choose. That's Ellie's tragedy. It's not just that Joel lies—everyone lies—it's that this particular lie leaves her suspended between love and resentment, between connection and anger, and unable to fully hold onto either end of the rope.

But Ellie wants to forgive Joel. She does. We hear it in her voice in that now famous porch scene. This fact is what makes Ellie's story so devastating. Reconciliation and forgiveness fall just short, though being a process, she was well on her way. They just don't have the time to get there before Joel is taken from her.

And so, Ellie chases ghosts. Not just Joel's, but the ghost of a life that fulfilled a meaning. "I was supposed to die in that hospital," she yells.[6] And at that moment she means it. Her purpose is stripped from her and she becomes infected, just not with *Cordyceps,* but the potential for vengeance. Joel's death lights the fuse that has been patiently biding its time.

In *Part II*, we watch Ellie lose everything. Dina. JJ. Her ability to play Joel's final gift. But it's not until she is on a beach in Santa Barbara, deep in salt, sand, and blood, that she sees the truth: Vengeance never restores what has been taken. It only ensures you lose everything that's left.

So, she lets go. The fingers that remain unclench. She releases Abby not because she's suddenly okay, but because she finally realizes she will never be okay if she doesn't. She chooses mercy, and in doing so, she saves herself as much as she saves Abby.

Will Ellie and Dina reconcile, though? Will she ever feel whole again? We don't yet know and that's not quite the point. The point is that she makes a choice to walk away and stop the cycle of violence that has been infecting humanity since foundation of the world. It doesn't kick down the door, but it does crack it open long enough to let a little light in. And for what it's worth, I think that's a type of truth of its own. The kind of truth that isn't about journalistic facts or literal history—though these things *are* important—but a kind that's about what is morally, ethically, philosophically, and even spiritually *real*. The kind of truth that says mercy is always stronger than vengeance, and that to let your enemy live is, paradoxically, how *you* begin to live again.

Which reminds me (and forgive me, I can't help myself): in *The Lord of the Rings*, Frodo doesn't save Middle-earth by killing Gollum. In fact, the truth of the matter is he "fails" miserably. He claims the Ring for himself and it's only through Gollum's fall—and Frodo's prior mercy toward him—that saves the Quest. Bilbo's pity. Frodo's restraint. That's where deliverance is found.

Likewise, in *The Last of Us*, it's mercy that saves Ellie. And though this isn't a clean, full, and neat restoration, it's enough to spare her from the absolute bottom. Time will tell if this will be enough to start again, but because we all love Ellie so much, we must have hope in her ultimate redemption, whatever that may mean to us.[7]

## TRUTH, IF WE CAN BEAR IT

> "Three things cannot be long hidden:
> the sun, the moon, and the truth."
>
> **— THE BUDDHA**

One of the main premises of this book is that the world of *The Last of Us* never gives us clean answers. It doesn't hand out tidy resolutions wrapped neatly in narrative bows, nor does it ever leave us to the comfortable confines of moral binaries. Instead, it does what many stories fail to do, which is to be honest. While many tales attempt to tidy up all the loose ends, this one leaves us with nothing but messiness. In this way, it's a fictional world as close to real as it gets. In this way, it's "true."

Joel's lie may have been born of love, but it still builds a wall between him and the one person he desires to protect. Ellie's obsession with the truth fractures her from Dina, from Jackson, and from herself. And yet, at the very end, with the ocean thrashing behind her and Abby drowning beneath her, Ellie finally makes a decision that isn't about truth or lies or vengeance, but about mercy. And mercy, as I alluded to earlier, is its own kind of truth. Not because it explains the past in any way, but because in letting go of the need for vengeance, mercy opens the possibility of a future not completely determined by what has already been lost.

And look, while I may have pooh-poohed the Buddhist dictum that the end of suffering is as simple as accepting impermanence and letting go of desire, they may be onto something with their Four Noble Truths. Because while Ellie may never be able to let go of Joel, on the beach in Santa Barbara she is, at last, able to let go of the idea that vengeance will bring peace. She lets the lie die. Not just Joel's lie, but her own. The lie that says justice and retribution are the same thing. That healing requires someone else to hurt.

But even that mercy—raw and redemptive as it may be—isn't the true ending of her story. Because the truth Ellie seeks isn't just about what happened in Salt Lake City or even why Joel lied. It's about what he means to her and what they mean to each other.

That's why the porch scene lingers the way it does. It's not a cinematic moment or a dramatic reveal. It's two people sitting in the dull glow of a porch light, trying to name something unnamable. "I don't think I can ever forgive you," Ellie says, "but I'd like to try."[8] And that, right there, is the truth she's after. It's not some sterile fact about who did what, but the painful, honest attempt to bridge a gap that should never have been there in the first place.

That moment on the porch is everything. Because even if Joel never fully earns her forgiveness, Ellie still reaches toward it. Not out of obligation, not because she's supposed to, but because some part of her knows that forgiveness, like truth, is the only thing that might set her free.

And so, when Ellie lets Abby go, it isn't because she suddenly finds peace. It's because she remembers what she was reaching for all along. Not closure. Not justice. But the chance to stop lying to herself. To stop pretending that revenge can heal, or that silence can protect. To stop believing that anything short of the truth—if we can bear it—will ever be enough.

*9*

# IT CAN'T BE FOR NOTHING

*The Paradox of Redemption*

"*After all we've been through. Everything that I've done. It can't be for nothing.*"[1]

— ELLIE WILLIAMS

The desire for redemption can be a hell of a force. As less-than-angelic beings, it is something we all find ourselves in need of at one point or another.[2] The belief that our mistakes and regrets aren't what define us is crucial to our own contentment, that no matter how deep we've sunk, there's still a ladder leading back toward the light. In most stories, the ladder is sturdy, predictable, and safe. A character screws up, learns a valuable lesson, makes a sacrificial gesture, and voilà! Redemption arc complete. Roll credits. Cue the slow orchestral theme in G minor.[3]

Take *Star Wars*, for example. Not the Disney+ flavor of the week or whatever the hell Palpatine's clone is supposed to be.[4] I'm talking the OG trilogies! Anakin Skywalker, once the galaxy's genocidal maniac in a cape, redeems himself in a single act: saving his son and chucking the emperor down a bottomless pit. He dies moments later in Luke's arms, unmasked and truly *seen*. Not as Darth Vader, the machine. But as Anakin, the father. The man. The one who, even after everything, gets to tell Luke that he has, at last, been "saved."[5]

Even in gaming, where moral ambiguity tends to run deep, redemption still gets top billing. I mean, it's literally in the title of the *Red Dead Redemption* series. And nowhere is it more poignantly explored than in the story of Arthur Morgan. For most of the game, Arthur is a violent outlaw—robbing trains, intimidating homesteaders, and leaving behind a trail of bodies in the name of loyalty to the van der Linde gang. But when he contracts tuberculosis and realizes his time is short, something shifts. The violence doesn't disappear, but a conscience begins to emerge. He starts making amends, not just spiritually, but tangibly. He helps Edith Downes, the widow of a man whose death he has indirectly caused. He risks his life to provide John Marston and his family with a way out of the gang life.[6] In short, he becomes someone who gives more than he takes. His redemption is neither sanitary nor fully complete, but it *is* honest. And that honesty is what makes it resonate.

This type of redemptive story is emotionally satisfying and beautiful, but it's not always how things work in the real world. And it is especially not how things work in *The Last of Us*.

This is a universe where there are no grand gestures setting things to right, no last-minute saves that wash away decades of violence, and no emotionally tidy deathbed scenes that send you out of the theater with your faith in humanity partially restored. Instead, Naughty Dog gives us a man in Joel who loves deeply, lies constantly, kills indiscriminately, and yet, still earns our affection. Or, at least our understanding. So, maybe that's the real question here: Does Joel ever find redemption? Is he ever not just some "shitty person" who does a lot of fucked-up shit? Or does he, like Anakin, get to undergo one final transcendent act that lets us see past the armor?

To get to these answers, we must understand how this world treats redemption. (Spoiler: it's not kindly.) Unlike stories that frame redemption as a destination—something to be earned through penance and self-sacrifice—*The Last of Us* presents us with something much messier, if it is to be attained at all.

This chapter is about such a tension, about what it means to seek wholeness in a world where everything is fractured and torn. We begin with Joel's "other daughter," Ellie, whose pursuit of justice becomes a downward spiral of grief and trauma, before turning to her mimetic mirror, Abby. Abby stops trying to earn redemption, yet ironically finds it by simply choosing to care for someone else. Finally, we circle back to Joel, who might not ever make amends for what he has done, but who finally lets himself be loved anyway.

## TWO OPPOSING FORCES

### Ellie's Spiral and the Limits of Redemption

If *The Last of Us* were interested in a simple story about the power of redemption, we would have long since witnessed Ellie admit wrongdoing and perform penance before walking into the sunset, her head held high. She would have ended up at home with Dina, singing to JJ on Joel's old guitar. But this is *The Last of Us*, not *Les Misérables*, and the path Ellie walks, contrary to that of Jean Valjean, isn't paved with moral clarity or a redemptive arc that wraps itself in a neat bow. It's a road littered with broken promises, shattered relationships, and a near religious devotion to the lie that pain can be fixed by causing more of it.

We're conditioned, narratively, to expect a turning point. For a story to "work," we say, there must be some moment where the protagonist wakes up, says "enough," and begins the slow and painful crawl toward healing. Ellie doesn't get that moment. Not really (or perhaps "not yet," if there is to be a *Part III*). Yes, she chooses to spare Abby at the end of *Part II*, but everyone who has played through the horror that is the beach scene knows there's a hollowness to it, like a muted cry into the void. Nora is still dead. Owen, Mel, and their unborn child are still dead. Jesse is still dead. Dina has already gone. And JJ? He probably won't even remember her.

That's the thing about vengeance. As we explored in chapter 7, it has a way of chewing through everything you love long before it ever gets to the person you blame. Joel believes he can lie to Ellie and save her from pain so she can live a "normal" life in Wyoming. Ellie believes she can kill her way to a type of closure that will, in some desperate way, bring Joel back to life. Both are wrong, even though both believe, at the time, they are doing the right thing. Which is why one of the themes of this book is that love can indeed inspire some of the most morally fraught decisions imaginable.

If there's any redemption for Ellie, then, it isn't in the sparing or the killing. Rather, it *starts* with the leaving—but it's only a start! On that beach in Santa Barbara, she finally lets go. Of Abby. Of Lev. Of the lie that vengeance could ever heal her. And while Ellie's letting go doesn't fix anything, it does stop the bleeding (if only for a moment). Whether that moment leads to anything more, we don't know. And that's what haunts and makes me half hope a *Part III* is never made. Because this world doesn't promise happy endings, and some characters' relationships stay broken. But if this is the last we see of Ellie—walking away, empty but alive—then we will have to live with the fact that we can never know for certain whether she discovers complete redemption. She gets only a taste of it in her refusal to finish Abby off, but like a melody that fails to find a resolve, we are left wondering what her next chord will be.

## Abby: A Quiet Kind of Redemption

When we first meet Abby, she is defined entirely by vengeance. She's Joel's executioner, the product of a trauma so raw it has shaped her body, her identity, and her entire purpose. She doesn't just desire revenge, she trains for it constantly. She lives and breathes it. And for a time, she believes it will ultimately set things right.

But, of course, Joel's death doesn't give her the resolution she so desires. He dies in the mountains near Jackson, but Abby's void remains. Her nightmares continue and her relationships crumble. It's not until her hellish descent into the hospital basement to face off against the Rat King where things finally shift. Abby moves from avenger to protector, not for her own sake, but for someone else's. It's fitting, then, that her arc becomes less about vengeance and more about caretaking. Lev (and Yara, to a degree) becomes her compass, and as she chooses the children over the WLF, security, and even her own life, Abby begins to reclaim something she didn't even know she'd lost.

Her escape from the Rattlers' pillars with Lev in tow isn't a grand, redemptive victory, nor is it a cinematic payoff or narrative resolution. It's a battered woman and a traumatized kid rowing away from yet another ruin, toward a place that may or may not exist. And yet, it's the closest thing we get to hope.

Abby doesn't earn forgiveness from those she's harmed, nor does she get much in the way of closure or applause. Instead, what she earns is a sliver of freedom. A second chance. A possibility that she hasn't had in what probably feels like forever. Not because her story—or any story within *The Last of Us* universe—necessarily bends toward justice, but because she *bends herself* toward something other than revenge. And maybe that's what redemption really is. It's not the erasure of guilt or the undoing of harm with a single self-sacrificial act. It's the quiet, stubborn decision to live differently, for as long as that is, on the other side of it.

## THE PARADOX HOLDS

Not all stories provide a clean redemptive arc, though it tends to be the norm throughout modern storytelling. *The Last of Us* adds itself to a growing chorus of voices that prove it is anything but. Ellie and Abby stand as mimetic mirrors, each shaped by grief and vengeance, each carrying out brutal acts in the name of love, and each losing nearly everything along the way. Whereas

Ellie ends *Part II* in isolation and uncertainty, Abby rows toward a possible future with the boy who has taught her how to truly love, and perhaps more importantly, how to *be* loved again.

Again, neither arc fits the traditional storytelling mold. Ellie's act of mercy doesn't restore what she's lost. Abby's survival doesn't undo what she's done. And Joel? That's the question we started with. Does he ever find redemption? Or is he forever a man that spares (and lies to) Ellie while in his mind condemning everyone else? If loving a person so fiercely you damn the rest of the world is seen as an act of goodness, it's the kind that leaves a body count. Not an indiscriminate lineup of unnamed and faceless NPCs, but of real people with real friends and loved ones. And if it's nothing more than Ayn-Randian selfishness, it's the kind that wears the mask of altruistic devotion.

Both the brilliance and cruelty of Joel's story is that we're never given the catharsis of seeing him truly reckon with his choices. Other than some hints from his porch in Jackson, he doesn't have anything that resembles a Jean Valjean moment of confession or Anakin-style last breath where he saves the galaxy and makes peace with his son. Joel dies violently, not yet forgiven by Ellie, with his past catching up to him in the form of a golf club. This leaves us wondering if he would have ever fully faced what he had done, or if he'd gone to his grave clinging to the belief that he was objectively right. The closest we get to his repentance is that final flashback, where Ellie tells him, "I don't think I can ever forgive you… but I'd like to try."[7] It's a moment that cracks the door to redemption open just enough to let light spill in, only for death to slam it shut before either of them can walk through.

And therein lies the paradox: redemption, if it truly exists at all, is not a finish line. It's not even a guarantee. It's a trajectory that is kicked off by a 180-degree change in thinking. A choice to step away from the fire before it consumes you. Ellie makes that choice on the beach and Abby makes it in the theater (at the behest of Lev[8]). But Joel? His arc ends before we can see if he was ever capable of making such a choice.

## REDEMPTION...
## IF WE CAN CALL IT THAT

"God creates out of nothing. Wonderful you say. Yes, to be sure, but he does what is still more wonderful: he makes saints out of sinners."[9]

— **SØREN KIERKEGAARD**, *Journals and Papers*

Every religion worth its salt has its own version of the redemption story: atonement, salvation, enlightenment, karmic balancing. And yet, when you strip away the poetry, too many of these visions get boiled down to formulas and transactions. Do the right thing. Say the right prayer. Perform the right ritual. Alakazam! You are now redeemed.

Life's not like that, though. It is messy. Sometimes the damage can't be undone and the people you've harmed never forgive you. That's what *The Last of Us* understands, and why its version of redemption feels quite rare in storytelling.

Don't get me wrong, I love *Star Wars*. I think Anakin Skywalker's final act of redemption is one of the greatest moments in all of fiction. But his transformation feels too clean and archetypal. It's a great conclusion, of course, but very much tied up in a bow. We can't let that be the only version of the story we tell ourselves, however, because most of us will never be afforded the opportunity to make one grand gesture that erases all the harm. Most of us, like Ellie, Abby, and Joel, will have to live with the messes we've caused for all our days.

But we should also have hope, for to be truly free is to accept this often-inconclusive fate. Redemption isn't about erasing the past or earning a divine stamp of approval; it's about whether you keep walking forward without letting the weight of what you've done crush you. It's about small acts like choosing mercy over vengeance and choosing to forgive others for your own sake. *The Last of Us* doesn't give us a story where everyone is saved, but it does give us a story where, despite the ruin, some still try to do the right thing.

## 10

# YOU CAN'T DENY THE VIEW

*Resilience, Rot, and the Life that Grows After Us*

> *"It's got its ups and downs. But...*
> *you can't deny the view though."*[1]
>
> — ELLIE WILLIAMS

It might seem strange to close a book on *The Last of Us* with a chapter on ecology. After all, most people come to these games for the story, the characters, and the carnage. They do not pick up their controllers just to gawk at the plant life creeping over the crumbling skyscrapers. But like I did with both *The Wisdom of Hobbits* and *Mimetic Theory & Middle-earth*, taking it back to the land was always where we were headed. I can't help it. I'm a farmer. A permaculturist. A very tall Hobbit. I spend my days with dirt under my nails, knowing firsthand that life is life regardless of whether we're here to witness it. And if we don't appreciate the growing things all around us, we don't deserve them.

Nature doesn't give a good goddamn about our cities or our borders, our headlines or our hashtags. It doesn't pause to grieve our wars. It doesn't even flinch at our extinction. (Hell, it may even be cheering it on, given how parasitic we've become.) One of the quiet themes of my introduction to this book was the resilience of the natural world, the idea that it exists with or without our consent. In this final chapter, we circle back to those themes, because in the world of *The Last of Us*, as in our own, we might like to think we have the final word, but things don't work that way. The real endgame here is that the natural world doesn't care about who survives, or who gets their revenge, or even who finds redemption; the only pertinent question it seeks to ask is, "What grows next?"

## THE TRAGIC BEAUTY OF RUIN

There's a moment early in *Part I* when Joel and Ellie stop on their way through a broken Boston. The skyline is fractured and the streets are buckled. Everything is but a broken skeleton of human ambition being eaten on all sides and by every shade of green. And in the middle of all that collapse and ruin, life is teeming. Ivy cascades over steel girders. Trees push up through asphalt. Nature has broken the lock on the door we thought we had closed on it, and now it's pouring in unapologetically.

Ellie takes it all in, her voice subtly quieter than usual: "You can't deny the view."[2]

It's an odd thing to say, given everything that has been going on in their world—the dead bodies, the smell of rot, the ache of misery. But maybe this paradox is the point. In the ruins of our cultural mastery, the earth has done what the earth has always done: endure. Nature has no interest in our approval, no stake in whether we notice its persistence. And yet, standing atop our crumbled infrastructure, we can't help but notice it. Because there's beauty here. Raw. Uninvited. Inconvenient beauty.

Again, that's the contradiction I keep coming back to: how life thrives in the cracks of our failures. How even when our cities fall and our systems collapse under the weight of their own hypocrisy, there is a kind of resurrection that happens without us (and often despite us). The question for *us*, then, isn't whether life will continue after we are long gone. We know it will. The question is what can life teach us *now*... about endurance, about decay, about the strange and almost offensive possibility of rebirth.

In a later section, we will discuss the theology of cycle and decay—what I'm labeling "compost theology"—but for now, let's step back and mention the science and symbolism of *Cordyceps*, and what it can teach us about our place in the world.

## THE SCIENCE AND SYMBOLISM OF CORDYCEPS

Before *The Last of Us* ever breaks our hearts with golf clubs and Taylor guitars, it terrifies us with what could very possibly become a real-world nature documentary. The opening premise is almost insultingly simple: What if an actual fungus that hijacks insect brains—*Ophiocordyceps unilateralis*, if you're into Latin—could somehow mutate to infect humans? In the natural world, *Cordyceps* infiltrates an ant, rewires its behavior, forces it to climb the stem of a plant, and then bursts out of its head to spread spores and begin the cycle again. It's part horror, part biology, and part reminder that nature doesn't give a fuck about consent.

In the video game series, *Cordyceps* is not a destroyer for destruction's sake, however. It's a biological process that transforms and consumes what already is, clearing the way for what might be. In this sense, the fungus itself is less of an immoral villain and more of an amoral grim gardener with a heavy hand and a naturally selfish survival instinct. That's the unsettling brilliance of this premise: decay isn't just about what rots, it's about what becomes renewed. Is the loss of human control framed as a necessarily "bad" thing? It depends on the lens through which you are looking. The skyscraper draped in ivy, the highway overtaken by wildflowers, the giraffes meandering through the ruins... these are not tragedies. They are reminders that our "dominion" has always been temporary, and probably overstated to begin with.

Which forces yet another uncomfortable question for us to wrestle with: If the world does better without us, what does that say about the way we've been living *with* it? Our obsession with unchecked capitalistic growth and with consumption as proof of success has left us fragile at best and fatalistically doomed at worst. The *Cordyceps* outbreak is fictional,[3] but the ecological truth behind it is not. Indeed, no human empire outruns the patient, relentless work of nature.

## Sin as Disconnection

In Christian theology, "sin" is often reduced to a moral checklist, a set of personal failings that either become forgiven by God or land you in eternal trouble. But if we take a less adolescent view of the concept, sin isn't so much about breaking rules but more about breaking relationships: with God, with each other, and with the land beneath our feet. Somewhere along the way, large swaths of humanity have traded the humility of stewardship for the arrogance of dominion, treating the planet not as a home and a garden, but as a warehouse and a factory. Heartbreakingly, its forests are reduced to nothing more than inventory, its oceans as dumping grounds, and its critters as resources for maximized profits.

Incidentally, when you live that far out of balance with nature, you start to mistake its correction for punishment. The *Cordyceps* outbreak feels like judgment because it strips away our illusion of control. But from another angle, the fungus is simply doing what living systems do: seeking equilibrium. We've been so long removed from planetary homeostasis that any movement back toward it feels like white-hot wrath. In reality, however, it's more like a forest fire clearing deadwood. Sure, it is brutal in the moment, but also necessary for renewal.

This is where the game's "rewilded eschatology" takes root. The apocalypse isn't an act of divinely-mandated destruction and retribution—no matter what the Seraphites might say—it's the inevitable rebalancing of a system we've pushed too far. And if that sounds harsh, it's only because we've forgotten what it means to belong here in the first place.

Tolkien, of course, saw this long before Naughty Dog coded spores and skyscrapers into our nightmares. After Saruman strips the forest of its trees and poisons the land with industry, Fangorn itself rises against him. The Ents don't burn with vengeance so much as they move with inevitability. Like any system out of balance, the land pushes back. Saruman's downfall comes not by sword or spell but by the trees themselves[4] reclaiming what has been stolen. It is a rewilding of Middle-earth, a reminder that even in fantasy, the natural world doesn't need us to defend it so much as it insists on its own correction.

## THE WORLD WITH OR WITHOUT US

### Rewilded Eschatology

In chapter 1 of this book, we talked about how every culture tells stories of the end. But in *The Last of Us*, the end of the world as we know it is strangely quiet and ironic. There is no fire and brimstone from above, no nuclear flash, no trumpet blast from heaven. Just fungal spores, spreading silently, remaking the world in their own image.

And what comes after the end? Not nothing. Never nothing. What comes after is the slow green hand of rewilding. Vines where we've poured concrete. Wolves where we paved highways. Accidental orchards where suburbs collapsed under their own mountains of debt.

We've seen this play out before. The Chernobyl Exclusion Zone (CEZ) has witnessed a resurgence of gray wolves.[5] Wild boars are running rampant in Fukushima. It's eerie, yes, but also strangely beautiful. As though the planet has been holding its breath for centuries, waiting for us to step aside. The twist is we see this as tragedy and call it apocalypse, but the wolves don't. The boars don't. The vines don't. The world doesn't mourn our absence. It just shrugs (or maybe sighs with relief) and continues moving on.

## Compost Theology

If rewilding is what the earth does in our absence, compost is what it does with our remains. Death is never the end in any natural system. Rather, it's the raw material needed to create new life. Or, to put it this way: rot is not waste; it's alchemy.

That's true biologically,[6] but it's also true spiritually. Every grief, every mistake, every loss we carry can eventually break down. Pain, if we don't clutch it like Gollum clutches the Ring, becomes soil for something else. Sometimes it takes years, sometimes a lifetime, but even the ugliest refuse can feed new growth.

For many of our favorite characters, this "something else" never comes. But the model is there, and it's what makes *The Last of Us* such a profoundly ecological story, one from which we can discover many truths. For instance, if we accept that our failures will not vanish into a void, we can accept that they have the ability to enrich the ground we stand on. Trauma doesn't disappear, but it can slowly and almost invisibly nurture mercy, humility, and even hope. This means the apocalyptic landscapes of *The Last of Us* are not meant to simply terrorize us, but to instruct. We can learn that endings are just beginnings, provided we're willing to let what's dead stay in the ground long enough to feed whatever comes next.

I see this truth play out every day on my farm in Northern California. The weeds we rip up, the stalks that collapse after harvest, the kitchen scraps, the chicken manure... all of it goes into piles that at first look like refuse. But give it time, give it rain and sun and worms and the slow patience of the soil, and what was once garbage becomes the richest matter on the farm. Black, teeming, and fertile.

And if death becoming life is true of soil, why wouldn't it also be true of us? All our suffering, not erased or forgotten, but composted into something that might one day nourish mercy or gentleness or even the courage to begin again.

Indeed, *The Last of Us* takes us deeper than the Mines of Moria and into the darkest rot of human trauma, but it never leaves us there without the faint smell of soil. And in doing so, it reminds us that even what was meant for harm, even what is ugly beyond recognition, can in time nurture something better, if we will only allow it.

## THE SACRED IN WHAT REMAINS

> "Ask the beasts and they will teach you the beauty of this earth."
>
> — ST. FRANCIS OF ASSISI

If the final ecological takeaway is that we should cultivate and care for the planet in order to survive, the deeper lesson is that we must also learn from it. Once we stop treating the earth like a backdrop to our story and start receiving it as a teacher, something sacred opens. God, if we can even use such a word, is not found in the heavens we try to escape to, but in every space that flows between every fungal network running silently beneath all our feet, and in the hush of snow on rooftops in Wyoming, and especially in the stubborn mercy of Ellie finally walking away from vengeance. The divine isn't "above" the rot; it's *in* the rot, transforming it into fertile soil.

Mystics like Julian of Norwich and Hildegard of Bingen knew this truth long before a PlayStation ever hummed to life. Divinity reveals itself not in fleeing the mess but in inhabiting it. Pierre Teilhard de Chardin called it the Christ who animates evolution itself[7] while the ancient Greeks labeled it the *Logos*.[8] But whatever labels one puts on it, the idea is that true divinity is found in the God who doesn't abandon the world—though it sometimes appears that way—but binds it together, cell by cell, root by root. In this sense, love itself is ecological. It spreads, roots, clings, regenerates, and in a world as dark as *The Last of Us*, constantly adapts.

I've said it throughout this book, but it bears further repeating: maybe the paradox at the heart of both the games and our own fragile lives is that we are never freed from the world or from our wounds, but only within them. Redemption, forgiveness, mercy... none of these arrive as clean victories. They come instead like compost beneath calloused hands: slow and quiet, yet obstinate and unrelenting.

Which brings us back to that moment overlooking the ruined city of Boston, when Ellie breathes, "You can't deny the view."[9] After everything we go through in life, my hope is that there's still a vista worth pausing for, that life and love win. But not though force or coercion—through rewilding and composting, forgiveness and mercy.

The truth of the matter is that life doesn't wait for us to catch up, to make peace, to figure out what it all means. It simply keeps going, rooting through the cracks of our ruins, and threading itself into the very places we thought were barren. If *The Last of Us* teaches us anything, it's that survival isn't the pinnacle but the baseline. What matters is what comes after—whether we can grow, adapt, and cultivate something worth leaving behind.

Indeed, we are never separate from the land. We rise and fall with it. Our wounds feed its soil, while its soil, in turn, offers us a future. If redemption exists at all, it will not be found in vengeance or control, but in learning to live as part of the same ecology we once believed we could dominate.

So yes, be like Ellie and take notice of the broken skyline, with vines spilling down its sides and giraffes wandering through the wreckage. You can't deny the view. But more than that! You can't deny the lesson. The earth is telling us a story more ancient than any of our myths; we just need to open our ears, our minds, and our hearts, and listen.

# Epilogue

*Take On Me: Finding Hope in the Ruins*

*"I struggled for a long time with surviving. And you... No matter what, you keep finding something to fight for."*[1]

— JOEL MILLER

Hope is a strange note to end on. Especially here. Especially in a world like *The Last of Us*, where hope always feels a little out of place, a little too fragile, like a candle burning against the wind. Yet hope is there, tucked between the cracks of all the ruin. You hear it in the soft strum of Joel's guitar, in the way Ellie longs to forgive her father-figure, in the laughter of kids playing in a snowy Jackson. And yes, even in a somber rendition of "Take on Me" played to Dina in an abandoned music store. For one fleeting moment, apocalypse doesn't have the final word. Music does. Love does. Life does.

That scene, devoid of the story's near-constant violence and vengeance, stands out like a scar that has healed smoother than the skin around it. Ellie's voice, uncertain but deceptively steady, offers something the game otherwise refuses us: the possibility that beauty can survive, even after everything else is ash and blood. Such beauty isn't permanent, but the point is that it happens at all. That's the thing about hope. It doesn't need to endure forever to be real. It just needs to show up.

Perhaps that's one last lesson for us today. Survival matters, but survival alone is not enough. To merely endure without hope, without joy, without the courage to love and laugh, is to miss the point of life entirely. In fact, survival without growth is closer to death than life. That is why the phrase "endure and survive," so often repeated throughout the games, is both true and insufficient. Yes, we must endure and survive. What other choice do we have? But if we stop there, we've given the infection the final word. What we need, and what Ellie, Abby, and Joel all stumble toward in their own fractured ways, is something more: *growth*. The willingness to rediscover, adapt, and create, even after losing everything.

I've written before—in *The Wisdom of Hobbits*—about the necessity of balance. Hobbits understand it better than most, how life is a dance between comfort and adventure, between the garden and the road. They grow to understand how you cannot live forever in the safety of the Shire, but neither can you live always in peril and conflict. Growth requires both rootedness and risk, home and horizon. As my best friend Michael Machuga has stated, growth requires both an adventure and a home (preferably one with a roaring fire, something warm in your cup, and a place to put up your furry Hobbit feet).[2] The problem in *The Last of Us* is that outside of Jackson, its characters are never afforded such balance. They are forever uprooted, forever forced to walk roads they did not choose, unable to plant themselves in the soil of something lasting and sustainable. The tragedy is not just in the characters' suffering, but in their inability to thrive.

Still, the aspiration remains. Survive and endure, of course. But toward what end? The hard truth—perhaps the most human truth—is that to endure without finding a way to grow is to become less than fully alive, to become concrete statues of ourselves. And so, we watch Ellie grasp at vengeance because it feels like purpose, and we ache for her to see that there is another way. We watch Abby drag Lev toward a future that may not exist, and we hope against hope that the journey itself becomes a kind of growth.

Growth, though, does not mean the absence of loss. It never has. To grow is to accept that loss is woven into the fabric of existence. Joel loses Sarah fifteen minutes into the game, but he later finds Ellie. Abby loses her father, but she finds Lev. Ellie loses Joel, then Dina, then nearly herself. Loss is constant, but it is not the whole story. Because while some losses cannot be replaced, there always exists the possibility of rediscovery. Joel discovers his heart again. Abby discovers a tenderness that surprises even her. Ellie, even in her desolation, discovers the courage to stop the cycle of violence. And rediscovery, though it never gives back what has been taken, does give us the chance to be something different on the other side of grief.

This is why empathy and compassion matter so much. They are not sentimental extras to tack onto survival. Rather, they are the very soul of what makes survival worth anything. If we endure without compassion, we may live, but we will not be alive. We will be shells, emptied of what makes us human. *The Last of Us* insists that moments of compassion—the giraffes, the jokes from Ellie's pun book, Joel's quiet promise to teach her guitar, Lev's kindness to Abby—these are not filler, but the entire point of the story. Moments like these remind us that love is what turns endurance into life. That empathy is what transforms survival into hope.

The natural world knows this balance better than we do. I'm reminded of it every day on my farm, where rot is never the end and decay is always an opening. Compost sometimes stinks, but it always feeds. The weeds that choke a path today may be groundcover protecting tomorrow's soil. Death itself, which we so often treat as an interruption, is simply part of the pattern that makes life possible. That's not optimism; it's science. The same truth that makes ivy, lichen, and all manners of shrubbery thrive after our cities collapse is the one that makes mercy possible after vengeance, or hope possible after despair. The world doesn't give up on itself, and neither should we.

And maybe the deepest revelation found in this story is that life wins. Not through strength. Not through control. Not through domination or vengeance or the illusion that we can make the world bend to our will. Life wins in quieter ways. It wins through fungi, forgiveness, and fields breaking through the ruins of what we built. Through songs sung in abandoned music stores, hands held in the dark, and the stubborn insistence that love still matters, even when everything else is crumbling.

It is fitting, then, that Ellie ends *Part II* not with triumph, not with neat resolution, but with a walk into the unknown. She is not redeemed, not whole, not finished. But she is moving. And maybe that is enough for now. Because in this world, like in ours, closure can be a bitter myth. What we get instead is the possibility of growth, if we're willing to reach for it.

I admit, part of me hopes Naughty Dog proves me wrong in *Part III*. I hope Ellie finds something like redemption, something like peace, something like the life she glimpsed on her and Dina's farm. But if she doesn't find her peace—if she keeps wandering, searching, stumbling—it will only confirm what this story has been telling us all along: that hope is not a guarantee, but a gamble. That growth is not inevitable, but possible. And that possibility, fragile though it is, is enough to keep going.

"You can't deny the view," Ellie says in Boston, staring at the ivy-strangled skyscrapers. She's right. You can't. Not because it's easy or comforting, but because it's true. The ruins do not lie. They tell us that life persists, even when we do not. And if we are brave enough to see it, they also show us that survival is only the beginning. The end—if we let it—can be growth.

And in the end, that's what this book has ultimately been about. Not just the saints, or the sinners, or the clickers, but the strange and terrible and beautiful mixture of all three. *The Last of Us* shows us that love and loss cannot be disentangled, that to live is to lose, and that to lose is sometimes the only way we rediscover love again.

So have hope that no matter what circumstance you find yourself in—whether you're being chased by a horde of clickers or lied to by a fellow survivor you thought you could trust—there is life and life abundant on the other side of suffering.

   We are all saints.

   We are all sinners.

   May we all learn how to love despite our loss.

   And may we all rediscover our souls along the way.

# Endnotes

Preface

1. Not to brag or anything, but I once beat *Contra* without the now famous cheat code that every Millennial probably still knows: Up, Up, Down, Down, Left, Right, Left, Right, B, A, Start (or, if you're playing multiplayer, Select, Start).

2. The first two titles to use a form of speech were the arcade games *Stratovox* and *Berzerk*. However, the voicing was not recorded in the way it is today for the simple reason that there was not enough storage space. It wasn't until the advent of the CD-ROM when fully recorded dialogue could become the norm in gaming.

3. The development budget for the original *Super Mario Bros.*, for instance, is estimated to have been roughly $17,000.

4. Makuch, "Naughty Dog Founder Reveals Budgets of Original Games and Why They Sold to Sony," para. 6.

5. While C.S. Lewis once argued that the gates of hell are locked from the inside, *The Last of Us* shows us that this is not always the case.

6. As of writing this, I have completed three playthroughs and watched another two. The Prologue does not get any easier with each experience.

7. Naughty Dog, *Grounded II*, 1:56:56–1:58:35.

8. Valentine, "Neil Druckmann Says 'Don't Bet on' There Being a The Last of Us Part 3," para. 3.

9. In fact, one of my final proof editors for *The Wisdom of Hobbits* acknowledged that they had never read or watched *The Lord of the Rings* prior to editing my book, but once finished, immediately sat down to view the films, and later admitted to having a desire to read the entire series.

10. Not that you necessarily need cum jokes for a great story, it just helps.

11. Naughty Dog, *The Last of Us: Part I*, Jackson.

An Introduction to the End of the World

1. Naughty Dog, *The Last of Us: Part I*, Hometown.

2. Ibid., The University.

3. Ibid., Quarantine Zone.

4. Ibid., Pittsburgh.

5. The number of those murdered remains unknown.

6. Ibid. The Outskirts.

7. Ibid.

8. See Hope Pino's pendant, numbered "000318."

9. This is the official slogan of the WLF.

10. See "WLF Recruiter Journal," found in the upper floor of the Serevena Hotel.

11. See a handwritten note from Isaac Dixon to an unnamed FEDRA defector, which reads: "Everything is in place. We will be waiting. Once we intercept the convoy and take the FEDRA officers captive, you can abandon your post and join us. I know you've taken numerous risks and lived in fear of being discovered. Your loyalty to our cause is appreciated."

12. See multiple notes found throughout the city of Seattle, including, "Need a plan note," "Boris' confession," and "Condolence note."

13. The Seraphites are called "scars" because of the facial scars they all bear, given to them during their initiation into the Seraphite religion.

14. Naughty Dog, *The Last of Us: Part I*, Seattle Day 2 (Ellie).

15. Ibid. Paige's body can be seen hanged near her husband's, with her blood being used to make a mural of the insignia of the cult.

16. For example, the Seraphites hang their sacrificial victims by the neck as they disembowel them. After the sacrifice is made, they chant, "now they are free," as they celebrate their alleged atonement.

17. See a letter exchange between "Gray" and "Jules," which reads, "Despite what we heard, it was the WLF who broke the truce. We've been lied to, Jules." (Naughty Dog, *The Last of Us: Part I*, Seattle Day 2 [Ellie]).

18. Naughty Dog, *The Last of Us: Part I*, The University.

19. This not only includes human bites, but monkey bites as well. See "Firefly's recorder," found in the science building at Eastern Colorado University.

20. Naughty Dog, *The Last of Us: Part I*, Hometown.

21. As a musician, I must note how the soundtrack composed by Gustavo Santaolalla perfectly embodies this stark juxtaposition.

22. We will discuss this much further in chapter 10.

23. Anthropologist Ernest Becker, in his Pulitzer Prize winning book, *The Denial of Death*, argues that it is our fear of death that is the main catalyst to all human conflict—religious, political, or otherwise. For those interested, I discuss Becker's theory at length in chapter 3 of *From the Blood of Abel*.

Lost in the Darkness

1. Naughty Dog, *The Last of Us: Part I*, Bill's Town.

2. The term *deus ex machina* (Latin for "god from the machine") originates from ancient Greek theater, where playwrights would sometimes resolve otherwise unsolvable plotlines by lowering an actor playing a god onto the stage using a crane-like device. The god would then intervene to untangle the story's conflicts, often abruptly and with little narrative buildup. Over time, the phrase came to describe any contrived or artificial resolution in literature, film, or drama. For a modern example, think of the final fight scene from *Star Wars: The Force Awakens*, when suddenly the ground splits in two just before Rey is about to strike down Kylo Ren.

3. Tolkien, *The Return of the King*, 241.

4. See, for instance, Revelation 8:7.

5. See Matthew 12:36–37, John 5:21–25, and many others.

6. See the Buddhist text Nibbedhika Sutta (Anguttara Nikaya 6.63).

7. In addition to Jesus Christ, there are many historical accounts of people taking on or being referred to as a son of God. From Alexander the Great to Julius Caesar, familial relationships with the divine have always been commonplace.

8. Though I will mention how the Seraphites interpret the outbreak as divine punishment for humanity's sins.

9. Jones, "Joel's Choice," 8.

10. To borrow a phrase used by Gandalf in *The Lord of the Rings*.

11. We will discuss this theme at length in chapter 10.

12. I have spent years trying to convince dispensationalist Christians of this, mostly to no avail.

13. See Revelation 21.

14. On March 25, 1965, from the steps of the Alabama State Capitol and after having completed the third march to Montgomery, Dr. King stated, "How long? Not long, because the arc of the moral universe is long, but it bends toward justice."

15. The Four Horsemen of the Apocalypse from the chapter 6 of book of Revelation represent conquest, war, famine, and death, all horrors we bring upon ourselves, often in the name of God.

16. It is only alleged that this quote is from Orwell, but is not found in any known published work.

17. Naughty Dog, *The Last of Us: Part I*, The Outskirts.

18. Ibid.

19. This is the main thesis of Joseph Campbell's "hero's journey," and is a context I am quite familiar with (see chapter 4 of *The Wisdom of Hobbits*, as well as *Beauty in Ordinary Things*, coedited with Yvette Cantu Schneider).

20. Like the Orwell quote before, it is not known if or where Angelou said this. Rather, it is possible the quote is a summation of the poet's overall philosophy.

21. In Greek, the word *"euangelion"* (εὐαγγέλιον) means "good news," and is the word we translate to "gospel."

22. Naughty Dog, *The Last of Us: Part I*, Lakeside Resort.

23. This is the final word spoken in *Part I*, and is something we will discuss further in chapter 8 (Ibid., Jackson).

24. See Genesis 4:24.

25. This is ironic, given the derogatory name "scars" used for her perceived enemies.

26. Utilitarianism is a philosophy that says to be considered moral, we should always do the act that leads to the greatest good for the greatest number of people.

27. Solzhenitsyn, *The Gulag Archipelago, 1918–1956*.

28. Rather than being a direct quote, this is more likely a synopsis of something Tolkien said, purported initially by long-time friend, C.S. Lewis. It is part of a longer conversation between the two (as well as Hugo Dyson) that took place on September 19, 1931.

## Endure and Survive

1. Naughty Dog, *The Last of Us: Part I*, Hometown.

2. To date, I have written or cowritten nine books on the topic of Christian theology.

3. See my books *Heretic!* and *From the Blood of Abel*, most notably.

4. In *Saying No to God*, scholar Matthew J. Korpman makes a strong case that the Hebrew bible demands that followers of God say no to him when morally appropriate.

5. In Jewish thought, humans are believed to have two impulses or "yetzer." One is the *yetzer hatov* (the good disposition) and the other is the *yetzer hara* (the evil disposition).

6. See Oord's *God Can't*, Karris' *Divine Echoes*, or Bahl's *The Death of Supernaturalism*.

7. Though, I will note how science continues to accurately warn humanity of the impending doom caused by our greedy, irresponsible, and selfish treatment of the planet, as well as the fallout from climate change. So, in *that* way, perhaps science is indeed prophetic.

8. E.g., the Fireflies, "David," and the WLF.

9. For those less versed in the finer points of *Star Wars* lore, Obi-Wan's death isn't merely a tragic plot point or a narrative device meant to accelerate Luke's Hero's Journey. Instead, it's a deliberate act rooted in the metaphysics of the Force itself. In *A New Hope*, Obi-Wan allows Vader to strike him down, not out of defeat, but because he understands that relinquishing his physical form will enable him to merge more fully with the Force. *The Clone Wars* reveals that Yoda undergoes an arduous, mystical trek to discover this very ability: the transition into what fans call "Force ghosthood," a continued existence that transcends bodily limitation. In this light, Obi-Wan isn't simply removed from the story, he evolves within it, thus inhabiting a mode of being that allows him to guide Luke with more clarity and less constraint, even from beyond the "grave."

10. Naughty Dog, *The Last of Us: Part I*, Hometown.

11. The story of Frank and Bill varies significantly between the HBO series and the video games, including the way in which Frank dies. As such (and as stated in the preface to this book), when there are narrative differences, we will always opt to follow the game series over the television adaptation.

12. For a Girardian analysis that contrasts the scapegoating of Ellie with that of Frodo Baggins, see my essay, "A Tale of Two Scapegoats: Comparing and Contrasting the Surrogate Victimage of Frodo Baggins and Ellie Williams," in *Vingilot*, Winter 2024, Issue 4.

13. Naughty Dog, *The Last of Us: Part I*, The Outskirts.

14. Ibid., Jackson.

15. Weil, *Gravity and Grace*, 28.

16. Naughty Dog, *The Last of Us: Part I*, Lakeside Resort.

17. This is known as the Euthyphro Dilemma of Plato, who posits, "Is it good because the gods love it, or do the gods love it because it is good?"

18. Piper, "Why Was It Right," para. 2.

19. From Dylan Thomas' poem, "Do Not Go Gentle into That Good Night."

20. Bonhoeffer, *Letters and Papers from Prison*, 361.

Look for the Light

1. Naughty Dog, *The Last of Us: Part I*, Left Behind.

2. Ibid., Bill's Town.

3. Ibid., Tommy's Dam.

4. Ibid., Lakeside Resort.

5. Naughty Dog, *The Last of Us: Part II*, The Farm.

6. Although, shortly after writing the first draft of this book, Tottenham went on to win the Europa League, its first European championship in over forty years.

7. See 1 John 4:8.

8. For those wondering, there is no right answer, which is why we still ask it.

Something to Fight For

1. Naughty Dog, *The Last of Us: Part I*, The Firefly Lab.

2. See Augustine's writings against Pelagius, as well as *On the Grace of Christ and on Original Sin* and *The City of God*.

3. Also known as "absolute spontaneity." Kant introduces this idea in the Third Antinomy of his *Critique of Pure Reason*.

4. See Benjamin Libet's 1980s experiments, John-Dylan Haynes' study using fMRI to map parts of the brain during the decision-making process, Tyson Aflalo's study from the Andersen lab at Caltech, and many more.

5. Schopenhauer, *Essay on the Freedom of the Will*, 47.

6. On page 15 of *I See Satan Fall Like Lightning*, Girard writes, "If our desires were not mimetic, they would be forever fixed on predetermined objects; they would be a particular form of instinct. Human beings could no more change their desire than cows their appetite for grass. Without mimetic desire there would be neither freedom nor humanity."

7. Girard, *Things Hidden Since the Foundation of the World*, Book III. This is a term Girard coined to counter the idea that the human being is an autonomous *in*-dividual.

8. I cried even harder when Arthur dies toward the end of *Red Dead Redemption 2* than I did when Joel dies at the beginning of *The Last of Us: Part II*.

9. In later chapters, I will address this, as it is not my belief that the Fireflies would have actually accomplished anything of value in sacrificing Ellie.

10. Hart, *The Deliverance of God*, 253.

11. Tolkien, *Tree and Leaf*, 68.

12. In Genesis 4:23–24, Lamech says the following to his wives (yes, plural): "Adah and Zillah, hear my voice; you wives of Lamech, listen to what I say: I have killed a man for wounding me, a young man for striking me. If Cain is avenged sevenfold, truly Lamech seventy-sevenfold."

No Half Measures

1. Naughty Dog, *The Last of Us: Part I*, The Quarantine Zone.

2. Distefano, *The Wisdom of Hobbits*, 104.

3. Tolkien, *The Return of the King*, 83.

4. In an 1887 letter to Bishop Mandell Creighton, Lord Acton wrote the now famous line, "power tends to corrupt, and absolute power corrupts absolutely."

5. Tolkien, *The Fellowship of the Ring*, 300.

6. Ibid., 34.

7. See Genesis 6:5.

8. Girard, *Things Hidden Since the Foundation of the World*, 11.

9. Let us not forget how, like Abby, Ellie's first love, Riley, was also a Firefly.

10. Distefano, *The Wisdom of Hobbits*, 116.

Beyond the Horizon

1. Naughty Dog, *The Last of Us: Part I*, Tommy's Dam.

2. Genesis 2:18.

3. In fact, Girard contends that all societies begin with mediated violence against an "other." For my comments on this idea, see *From the Blood of Abel* and *Mimetic Theory & Middle-earth*.

4. No offense to anyone named Seth.

5. See Girard's *I See Satan Fall Like Lightning* and *Things Hidden Since the Foundation of the World*, as well as James G. Williams' *The Bible, Violence, and the Sacred*.

6. Both the Department of Defense and the Centers for Disease Control remain in operation after the outbreak, though for how long and in what capacity is not fully known.

7. We have seen this all throughout history. In the Old Testament, the Hebrew people escape the slavery of Pharoah and Egypt, yet use slave labor to build their first temple roughly 480 years later. Toward the beginning of the United States' founding, Roger Williams flees the Massachusetts Bay Colony to escape religious persecution from a group who had just fled Europe for the same reason. And today, Israel's government, with the financial backing of the United States, is, as of writing this, committing genocide against the Palestinians when not 100 years prior they faced their own extermination at the hands of the German Nazis.

8. In a personal email exchange with Lauren Cibene, she reminds me that, "*City of Thieves* isn't just a random book selection. It's intentional foreshadowing. [It] tracks the journey of two characters, a young man and a teen boy, who are inadvertently thrown together and forced to navigate the hellscape of occupied WWII-era Leningrad. In a corpse-littered city, they dodge cannibals, bombs, bullets, and evil leaders who punish with disfigurement and torture. Through all this, they learn to protect and care for each other like brothers. The teen boy in *City of Thieves* is named Lev, leaving us to wonder if Abby thinks back to this book when she meets her own Lev."

9. Naughty Dog, *The Last of Us: Part II*, Seattle Day 3.

10. I am not attacking anyone's faith here, nor any particular tradition. I am, however, referring to the perversion of various faiths across traditions. From the white Christian nationalists, to fundamentalist Jihadists, to the Hindu nationalist responsible for the death of Gandhi, there have been many manifestations of this kind.

11. Though we don't explicitly witness any firsthand accounts of other forms of prejudices, we can assume racism also still exists, even in Jackson.

12. Girard, *Things Hidden Since the Foundation of the World*, 287.

13. A good analogy for this can be found among the trees. In tropical areas that face severe wind and hurricanes, palms can be frequently seen surviving the damage. Why? Because they are far less rigid than other species of trees, and can handle bending and bowing in winds up to 145 MPH.

14. Naughty Dog, *The Last of Us: Part I*, Bus Depot.

You Can't Stop This

1. Naughty Dog, *The Last of Us: Part II*, Jackson.

2. The common consensus among most biblical scholars is that the first creation narrative runs from Genesis 1:1–2:4a, while the second runs from 2:4b–2:25.

3. Girard, *Things Hidden Since the Foundation of the World*, 11
4. In Girard's theory, the ultimate originary event is a hypothetical moment in human history marked by the emergence of language and culture. This event is signaled by a group's mediated violence against a chosen victim, all done to quell the flood of vengeance gripping the members of the group.
5. After prohibition and myth, the third and final pillar of culture, according to Girard, is ritual. This is a community's repeated effort to continue the peace that spawns from their collective violence against the scapegoat.
6. I do not mean to suggest that Cain and Abel (or Adam and Eve for that matter) are historical figures who literally walked the earth. Instead, like Romulus and Remus from Rome's origin story, they are all archetypal, representing universal patterns that can provide valuable insights for all people in all times and all places.
7. Genesis 6:11–12.
8. Genesis 6:13.
9. Naughty Dog, *The Last of Us: Part II*, Reveal Trailer.
10. One aspect of the game that goes further than most is that the NPCs we encounter have names, they have backstories, they have families. When you blow up a soldier and their dog, for instance, nearby enemies don't just take cover and come for you with everything they've got; they grieve their fallen comrades and cry out their names as well.
11. According to Strong's Exhaustive Concordance: *sōzō*; from a primary σώς *sōs* (contraction for obsolete σάος *sáos*, "safe"); to save, i.e. deliver or protect (literally or figuratively):—heal, preserve, save (self), do well, be (make) whole.
12. Aurelius, Marcus, *Meditations*.
13. Tolkien, *The Fellowship of the Ring*, 65.

Okay

1. Naughty Dog, *The Last of Us: Part I*, Jackson.
2. Also called the San Pedro Channel, this body of water is located between Long Beach, California, and Catalina Island.
3. Naughty Dog, *The Last of Us: Part I*, Jackson.
4. Naughty Dog, *The Last of Us: Part II*, The Farm.
5. Ibid.

6. Ibid.

7. We will explore the themes of redemption in the next chapter.

8. Naughty Dog, *The Last of Us: Part II*, The Farm.

It Can't Be for Nothing

1. Naughty Dog, *The Last of Us: Part I*, Bus Depot.

2. Most major world religions include a theology of redemption. In Christianity, redemption is often thought of as deliverance from sin and its consequences (i.e., death), while the Jewish Torah refers to it as the ransom of slaves (see Exodus 21:8). Islam emphasizes that to be "redeemed," a Muslim must have sincere faith and perform virtuous actions, such as praying and being charitable, while in Hinduism, a concept similar to redemption is called *prāyaścitta*, and it emphasizes not sin per se, but the liberation of guilt.

3. This is the key of John Williams' "The Force Theme."

4. I am not trying to throw shade at episodes 7, 8, and 9 for the sake of shade; I simply do not understand how many of the arcs from this trilogy fit into the larger *Star Wars* universe. With its rich tapestry of layered myths and deep lore, episodes 1–6 all fit seamlessly together and enhance one another, while the "Skywalker Saga" pays very little mind to any of it.

5. See *The Return of the Jedi*, where, after Luke pleads with his father to let him save him, Anakin admits, "you already have."

6. Ironically, in the original game, it is the United States government that thrusts John Marston back into a life of violence. Edgar Ross of the Bureau of Investigation kidnaps John's wife and son, forcing him to comply with the federal government's desire to rid the West of ruffians such as Bill Williamson and Dutch van der Linde.

7. Naughty Dog, *The Last of Us: Part II*, The Farm.

8. After Abby finds out from Ellie that Dina is pregnant, Abby, with her knife pressed against Dina's neck, says, "Good." Lev, beginning to tremble and cry, interjects: "Abby!" Which causes her to release Dina and walk away (Naughty Dog, *The Last of Us: Part II*, Seattle Day 3 [Abby]).

9. Kierkegaard, *Papers and Journals*, XI, I, A, 491.

You Can't Deny the View

1. Naughty Dog, *The Last of Us: Part I*, Bus Depot.

2. Ibid.

3. I make similar connections between Tolkien's fictional world and the ecological truths in front of us, especially vis-à-vis climate change. Tolkien used the story of Saruman, Treebeard, and the Fangorn Forest to warn us the dangers of industrialism, while Naughty Dog uses a mutated fungus to deliver similar truths about our present existential reality.

4. Just don't tell Treebeard I called him a "tree."

5. Some scientists have suggested these wolves may have developed some resistance to cancer, potentially due to natural selection in a radioactive environment.

6. On Happy Woods Farm—on any no-till farm, for that matter—compost is the most crucial component of our gardens.

7. de Chardin, "A Note on Progress," para. 31.

8. In Greek philosophy, the *Logos* (translated as "Word" in most Bibles) is considered to be the structuring principle of reality.

9. Naughty Dog, *The Last of Us: Part I*, Bus Depot.

Epilogue

1. Naughty Dog, *The Last of Us: Part I*, Jackson.

2. See *The Bonfire Sessions* and the foreword to *The Wisdom of Hobbits*.

# BIBLIOGRAPHY

Antonello, Pierpaolo, and Gifford, Paul, eds. *How We Became Human: Mimetic Theory and the Science of Evolutionary Origins*. East Lansing: Michigan State University Press, 2015.

Aurelius, Marcus. *Meditations*. Translated by Gregory Hays. New York: Modern Library, 2002.

Bahl, Chad. *The Death of Supernaturalism: The Case for Process Naturalism*. Chico: Quoir, 2025.

Beck, Richard. *The Slavery of Death*. Eugene: Cascade, 2013.

Becker, Ernest. *The Denial of Death*. New York: Free Press, 1973.

Bonhoeffer, Dietrich. *Letters and Papers from Prison*. Translated by Reginald H. Fuller. New York: Touchstone, 1997.

de Chardin, Pierre Teilhard. "A Note on Progress," in *Toward the Future*. London: HarperCollins, 1964.

Distefano, Matthew J. "A Tale of Two Scapegoats: Comparing and Contrasting the Surrogate Victimage of Frodo Baggins and Ellie Williams." In *Vingilot*. Winter 2024, Issue 4, 3–7.

———. *From the Blood of Abel: Humanity's Root Causes of Violence and the Bible's Theological-Anthropological Solution*. Orange: Quoir, 2016.

———. *Mimetic Theory & Middle-earth: Untangling Desire in Tolkien's Legendarium*. Chico: Quoir, 2024.

———. *The Wisdom of Hobbits: Unearthing Our Humanity at 3 Bagshot Row*. Chico: Quoir, 2023.

Druckmann, Neil, Mazin, Craig, et. al. *The Last of Us. Season 1*. January 15, 2023. HBO Max. https://play.max.com/show/93ba22b1-833e-47ba-ae94-8ee7b9eefa9a.

———. *The Last of Us. Season 2*. April 13, 2025. HBO Max. https://play.max.com/show/93ba22b1-833e-47ba-ae94-8ee7b9eefa9a.

Eliot, T.S. "The Hollow Men." In *T.S. Eliot: A Bibliography*. Edited by Donald Gallup. New York: Harcourt, Brace and Company, 1947.

Girard, René. *I See Satan Fall Like Lightning*. Translated by James G. Williams. Maryknoll: Orbis, 2001.

———. *Things Hidden Since the Foundation of the World*. Translated by Stephen Bann and Michael Metteer. Stanford: Stanford University Press, 1978.

Hart, David Bentley. *The Experience of God: Being, Consciousness, Bliss*. New Haven: Yale University Press, 2013.

Jones, Clint Wesley. "Joel's Choice: Apocalyptic Fantasies, Dystopian Hope, and the Post-Human Question." In Horn, Charles Joshua (ed.). *The Last of Us and Philosophy: Look for the Light* (The Blackwell Philosophy and Pop Culture Series). Stevens Point: Wiley Blackwell, 2024.

Karris, Mark Gregory. *Divine Echoes: Reconciling Prayer with the Uncontrolling Love of God*. Orange: Quoir, 2018.

Kierkegaard, Søren. *Papers and Journals: A Selection*. London: Penguin Classics, 1996.

Lucas, George, director. *Star Wars: A New Hope*. 1977; 20th Century Fox, 2011. Blu-ray disc.

———. *Star Wars: Attack of the Clones*. 2002; 20th Century Fox. Blu-ray disc.

———. *Star Wars: Revenge of the Sith*. 2005; 20th Century Fox. Blu-ray disc.

———. *Star Wars: The Phantom Menace*. 1999. 20th Century Fox. Blu-ray disc.

Lucas, George, and Kershner, Irvin, directors. *Star Wars: The Empire Strikes Back*. 1980; 20th Century Fox, 2011. Blu-ray disc.

Lucas, George, and Marquand, Richard. *Star Wars: Return of the Jedi*. 1983; 20th Century Fox, 2011. Blu-ray disc.

Makuch, Eddie. "Naughty Dog Founder Reveals Budgets of Original Games and Why They Sold to Sony." *Gamespot.com*. (January 6, 2025). https://www.gamespot.com/articles/naughty-dog-founder-reveals-budgets-of-original-games-and-why-they-sold-to-sony/1100-6528634/.

Naughty Dog. *Grounded II: Making The Last of Us Part II*. February 2, 2024. https://www.youtube.com/watch?v=SC3C7GMMfDU.

———. *The Last of Us: Part I*. Remastered. Sony Entertainment. 2022. PlayStation 5.

———. *The Last of Us: Part II*. Remastered. Sony Entertainment. 2024. PlayStation 5.

Oord, Thomas Jay. *God Can't: How to Believe in God and Love After Tragedy, Abuse, and Other Evils*. Grasmere: SacraSage, 2019.

Oya, Alberto. "Is Ellie's Revenge Ethically Justified?" In Horn, Charles Joshua (ed.). *The Last of Us and Philosophy: Look for the Light* (The Blackwell Philosophy and Pop Culture Series). Stevens Point: Wiley Blackwell, 2024.

Piper, John. "What Made It Okay for God to Kill Women and Children In the Old Testament?" *Desiring God*. (February 27, 2010). https://www.desiringgod.org/interviews/what-made-it-okay-for-god-to-kill-women-and-children-in-the-old-testament.

Schopenhauer, Arthur. *Essay on the Freedom of the Will*. Translated by Konstantin Kolenda. Mineola, NY: Dover Publications, 2005.

Shepard, Kenneth. "The Last of Us Show Tries to Change What the Game Told Us About Joel." *Kotaku*. (March 12, 2023). https://kotaku.com/last-of-us-tlou-hbo-show-finale-joel-lies-ellie-part-ii-1850209559.

Solzhenitsyn, Aleksandr. *The Gulag Archipelago, 1918–1956: An Experiment in Literary Investigation*. Translated by Thomas P. Whitney and Harry Willets.

Tolkien, J.R.R. *The Lord of the Rings: The Fellowship of the Ring*. New York: Ballantine, 1993.

———. *The Lord of the Rings: The Return of the King*. New York: Ballantine, 1993.

———. *The Lord of the Rings: The Two Towers*. New York: Ballantine, 1993.

———. *Tree and Leaf*. Edited by Christopher Tolkien. London: HarperCollins, 2001.

Valentine, Rebekah. "Neil Druckmann Says 'Don't Bet on' There Being a The Last of Us Part 3." *IGN*. (March 5, 2025). https://www.ign.com/articles/neil-druckmann-says-dont-bet-on-there-being-a-the-last-of-us-part-3.

Weil, Simone. *Gravity and Grace*. Translated by Emma Craufurd. New York: Routledge, 2004.

Watts, Alan. *Out of Your Mind: Tricksters, Interdependence, and the Cosmic Game of Hide-and-Seek*. Boulder: Sounds True, 2017.

Williams, James G. *The Bible, Violence, and the Sacred: Liberation from the Myth of Sanctioned Violence*. Eugene: Wipf & Stock, 2007.

To contact Matthew J. Distefano for speaking engagements, please visit www.quoir.com.

**Many Voices. One Message.**

*quoir.com*

www.ingramcontent.com/pod-product-compliance
Lightning Source LLC
LaVergne TN
LVHW041812060526
838201LV00046B/1229